FORWARD
IN THE FACE OF FEAR

My Life for Christ in the Muslim World

AN AUTOBIOGRAPHY OF MISSIONARY

Edgar Feghaly

First published in 2016 by Striving Together Publications, a ministry of Lancaster Baptist Church, Lancaster, CA 93535. Striving Together Publications is committed to providing tried, trusted, and proven books that will further equip local churches to carry out the Great Commission. Your comments and suggestions are valued.

Striving Together Publications
4020 E. Lancaster Blvd.
Lancaster, CA 93535
800.201.7748

Cover design by Andrew Jones
Layout by Craig Parker
Cover Photo by William Lofgren
Edited by Lesley Gonzalez

The author and publication team have given every effort to give proper credit to quotes and thoughts that are not original with the author. It is not our intent to claim originality with any quote or thought that could not readily be tied to an original source.

ISBN 978-1-59894-318-4
Printed in the United States of America

Dedication

To Pastor Garvan Walls, a faithful pastor and a great friend, who has daily prayed for us and whose church supported the missionary that came to Lebanon and led my family to the Lord.

CONTENTS

Foreword

To meet Edgar Feghaly is to meet a man who loves the Lord and loves people.

But what really stands out to me about both of these qualities is their quantity. Dr. Feghaly loves the Lord and the lost enough that he is willing to endanger his own life to preach the gospel in dangerous places.

In fact, when I think of Dr. Feghaly, I think of Paul's testimony in Acts 20:24, "But none of these things move me, neither count I my life dear unto myself, so that I might finish my course with joy, and the ministry, which I have received of the Lord Jesus, to testify the gospel of the grace of God."

This autobiography is riveting. It tells of a young boy reached for Christ—literally saved in the wake of a bomb explosion—and discipled in the faith. It tells of a young man whose heart burned with a desire to reach others for Christ, even when he was too young or it was too risky. It tells of a young father who, sensing God's call on his life to return to a war-torn country, went. It tells of a missionary committed to return to the young Christians in his care amid great danger. And it tells of the protective hand of God shielding His servant time and again.

These pages describe in engaging, understandable terms the complexities of Middle Eastern conflicts and the challenges they pose for Christians. They draw you in to the nuances of missions in Muslim areas.

But it's not just the experiences of Dr. Feghaly's life or the backdrop against which they're lived that make this book riveting. For woven throughout his story, you see the tapestry of how God molded and is using a life for His glory. You read of other lives changed—brands plucked out of the fire, churches planted in dark—even impossible—places, pastors trained to preach the gospel in areas where you and I assume there are no churches.

Above all, this book is riveting because it highlights the great power of the gospel of Jesus Christ. The gospel knows no boundaries of location, tradition, or belief systems. Christ is able to save to the uttermost all who come.

I'm thankful for a missionary like Dr. Edgar Feghaly who has committed his life to preaching the gospel in difficult places. I'm thankful for his love for Christ that causes him to not count his own life dear unto himself, and I'm thankful for his love for the lost that causes him to see himself as a debtor with no choice but to preach the gospel. And I'm thankful that this missionary is my friend.

Read these pages and be encouraged in the power of the gospel, challenged in the resource of prayer, and awed in the gracious, protective hand of God to further His work even in the very face of fear.

Paul Chappell
Lancaster, California
February 2016

Author's Note

In Lebanon, as in much of the Middle East, several groups are referred to as Christian who are not born again Christians. In many Middle Eastern countries, if you are born into an Orthodox or Catholic family, you are automatically considered a Christian and refer to yourself as such. Again, this does not refer to being a Christian in the Bible sense of the word but is used to differentiate culturally from being a Muslim. Throughout this book, I often use the terms as they are used in Lebanon. For instance, the Christian Lebanese Army (which is actually the same as the Lebanese Army) is not comprised of born again Christians, but calls themselves Christian because they are not Muslim.

ANYWHERE, PROVIDED IT BE FORWARD

I have always admired the Apostle Paul. One of the greatest men of faith in the Bible, Paul was used of God to write much of the New Testament and is known for his wide influence and bold proclaiming of the gospel throughout a thirty-year ministry filled with incredible victories as well as discouraging suffering.

Many things may be said about Paul, but no one can claim he was not focused. Through more trials and challenges than many of us will endure in a lifetime, Paul kept his eyes fixed on the Christ of Calvary as his Saviour, on Heaven as his future hope, and on the call of God on his life to bring others the good news of the gospel. And he urged other believers to have the same focus:

> *Wherefore seeing we also are compassed about with so*
> *great a cloud of witnesses, let us lay aside every weight,*

and the sin which doth so easily beset us, and let us run
with patience the race that is set before us, Looking unto
Jesus the author and finisher of our faith; who for the joy
that was set before him endured the cross, despising the
shame, and is set down at the right hand of the throne
of God.—Hebrews 12:1–2

Brethren, I count not myself to have apprehended: but
this one thing I do, forgetting those things which are
behind, and reaching forth unto those things which are
before, I press toward the mark for the prize of the high
calling of God in Christ Jesus.—Philippians 3:13–14

The Apostle Paul realized his life was not merely a collection of days and years he could spend frivolously, lured by distractions at every turn. He lived with the understanding that life was a race, and he wanted to finish it well: "But none of these things move me, neither count I my life dear unto myself, so that I might finish my course with joy, and the ministry, which I have received of the Lord Jesus, to testify the gospel of the grace of God" (Acts 20:24).

And near the end of his life, Paul indicated to Timothy that he had accomplished his mission: "I have fought a good fight, I have finished my course, I have kept the faith" (2 Timothy 4:7).

How was it that Paul could come to the end of his course with joy? It was because in the face of every adversity, every setback, every difficulty, Paul pressed *forward*. He refused to count his life dear to himself, but he counted the cause of Christ worthy of sacrifice.

More than once Paul wrote to believers and urged them to follow his example just as he followed the example of Christ (1 Corinthians 4:16; 11:1). So we can conclude from the testimony of Paul's life that we too are running a race as we strive to serve the Lord in what He has called us to do. And we too are called to press forward with focused intensity for Christ.

The story you will read in the following pages is the story of my race—not yet complete. The Lord has allowed me to serve in places of extreme upheaval—fraught with conflict, torn by wars, and destabilized by constant chaos. Each location has held its own causes for fear and reasons to turn back. But each location has also held unique opportunities for preaching the gospel and for offering eternal life to those who are seeing firsthand the brevity of temporal life. As God has given grace to continue in the face of fear, I've been privileged to see His gospel penetrate hardened hearts, and I've had the joy of seeing churches planted in dark, needy places.

God calls each of us to run our own race. We each face differing obstacles and setbacks, and we serve the Lord in various locations. Yet, regardless of where we serve or the exact capacity in which God has called us to labor for Him, we each must press forward for the Lord. I pray that my story will encourage you to know that God is faithful and that you can press forward even in the very face of fear.

Like David Livingstone, the nineteenth-century missionary explorer in Africa, may our motto be, "Anywhere, provided it be *forward.*"

One

THE MISSIONARY AND THE CROSSROADS

The Lebanese have always proudly declared their homeland is heaven on earth. Indeed, folk songs and stories describing the country's origins tell of a land that literally fell from heaven into the Middle East and later became known as Lebanon. Anyone questioning this claim is reminded that Lebanon is the only country in the world where one can find the magnificent "cedars of Lebanon" named in the Scriptures. The Lebanese argue that these particular cedars exist only in this land, and since the cedar was described also as the tree of God used in the building of His temple in Jerusalem (1 Kings 5:5–6), Lebanon must be part of Heaven.

As a Lebanese child raised during the 1950s, I grew up hearing these origin stories. And like the majority of the country, my family was also steeped in religion. At that time, about 60 percent of Lebanese citizens identified as nominal

1

Christians (Maronite Catholics and Orthodox). In our home, where my father was Maronite Catholic and my mother was Greek Orthodox, the word *Baptist* was unknown. Our community cared little for those of protestant and evangelical denominations; to us they were outcasts, infidels practicing what the Catholic priest described as illegal religions.

I attended a school owned by the Catholic church, and in addition to studying mathematics, science, history, and geography, my classmates and I took religion classes to learn the ceremonies, catechism, and traditions of the Maronite Catholic Church, which revolved around the lives of the Catholic saints (especially the Lebanese saints). We were taught to pray and to attend church in order to confess our sins to the priests. Every year, we were taken to the graveyard to pray for the dead, particularly that God would have mercy on our departed relatives. Most importantly, we were taught that because our God is very busy running the whole universe and cannot always find time to hear our prayers, every Christian must adopt a saint and pray to that saint to receive answers to prayer. We could bypass that saint by going straight to Saint Mary, who we were persuaded was almost equal to God. Saint Mary was the mother of God, the queen of Heaven, and the mediator through whom our prayers would be heard, filtered, and then conveyed to God. We understood Jesus was part of the trinity; we named Him whenever we made the sign of the cross, saying, "In the name of the Father, the Son (Jesus), and the Holy Spirit" and recognized that He suffered and was crucified. But Jesus was not as important as Saint Mary because He was only Mary's son.

Every year on Good Friday, the Maronite Catholic community watched "The Life of Christ" in movie theaters, and as a child, I cried with the rest of the people as we saw Jesus carrying the heavy cross after being beaten and tortured. It hurt us to see the blood gushing from His side and forehead. But we had no idea He suffered for us; nobody ever told us Christ died on the cross to open the gate to Heaven and save us. Instead, we focused on His mother, Mary, and how much she suffered. According to our church, she was the one who had to carry the pain of Christ's crucifixion in her heart. After all, wasn't that what Simeon meant when he told Mary, "(Yea, a sword shall pierce through thy own soul also,) that the thoughts of many hearts may be revealed" (Luke 2:35)?

Just a couple days later, during the special feast we held to celebrate Easter, we would greet each other with, "He is risen" and hear in response, "He is risen indeed." We never thought to question this ritual. The resurrection of Christ was simply another miracle. Mary did not need to be resurrected because she did not die; she went to Heaven alive.

We knew all about sin and its consequences, of course. Our religion teacher explained that committing a sin was not necessarily a problem because as long as we regularly visited the church confessional booth and confessed our sins to the priest, it was his duty to determine the appropriate penalty or penance we owed for our sins to be forgiven. After we died, we would approach the gate of Heaven and Saint Peter would be standing there with a scale in his hand. He would place our good works on one side of the scale and our bad works on the other side, and if the good outweighed the bad, we would be admitted to Heaven. But if the scale tipped in the other direction, we would be sent to Hell.

The fear of going to Hell was with me constantly as a child. Because I wanted desperately to go to Heaven and see Saint Mary, Jesus, and the other saints, I would wake up every morning and promise God that I would be a good boy. I promised I would pay attention in class, be polite to the other kids, and forgive the group of schoolyard bullies that often tormented me. Then I would get out of bed and get ready for the day, say good morning to my parents and brothers, and go to school with every intention of being well behaved; but it seemed I could never make it through a single day without breaking my promise. I soon developed a severe sense of guilt, realizing I could not meet the expectations of the church or do enough good works to outweigh my sins. Discouraged, I concluded there was nothing I could do to secure Heaven. I was seven years old, and I had already lost hope for my eternal future.

Hope for the Hopeless

My father supported our family for many years by operating a successful barbershop. His primary clients were the French army officers occupying Lebanon at the time, and they tipped generously; but when France granted Lebanon its independence and withdrew from the country in 1946, the shop could no longer sustain itself. My dad wisely decided to convert the space into a convenience store. My mom frequently assisted my dad in the store, and one day in 1956 as they worked together, a missionary named Clyde Aynes approached them to deliver an invitation to his storefront Baptist church nearby.

My dad politely declined. In his mind, and according to the teachings of Maronite Catholicism, all Protestants were infidels, so he wanted nothing to do with it. My mother, however, who was Orthodox and not Catholic, decided to attend a service and take her children with her.

My mom's decision was a result of the Lord preparing her heart many years before through the efforts of another missionary, an American named Miss Ford. That young woman had an amazing story of her own. Miss Ford was born into a wealthy family who worshipped the Lord, so when she contracted a virus in her childhood that left her crippled, they prayed earnestly along with her and their friends for God to heal her. When He answered their prayers, Miss Ford surrendered her life to be a missionary to the Middle East. In a time when women seldom traveled alone, she sailed to Palestine, landing in the Mediterranean seaport of Akka, which today is a part of Israel.

Miss Ford dove enthusiastically into ministry among the Syrian people. In time, she bought a donkey to travel to a region called Huron, into a town called Kharaba, inhabited by Druze Muslims and Orthodox Christians. There she met my mother's grandfather, an elder of Kharaba. He welcomed the gospel she brought, and, in spite of the opposition of others, he and many of his relatives received Christ as their Saviour. Later, my mother's father also embraced the faith, and though he remained Orthodox by identity, he and my grandmother attended the local Evangelical church that my great grandfather had been instrumental in building. My mother was not saved under Miss Ford's ministry, but a seed of the Word of God was planted in her life through the gospel's impact on her family, and at Clyde Aynes' invitation, that seed began to take root.

My mom asked my brothers and me if we would like to go to the Baptist Sunday school. At first, we were confused. We had heard of school on Monday through Friday, but what kind of school held classes on Sunday? My mother explained that Sunday school was quite different from Catholic school because we would hear stories from the Bible about the Lord God and Jesus. But the biggest difference was that unlike the teachers and priests at our Catholic school, the Baptists were kind and loving and would give us candy and show us movies. We were sold; to Sunday school we went.

We arrived at church that Sunday well-scrubbed, smartly dressed, and full of excitement, and were welcomed inside. We looked around in surprise. This simple converted storefront was no match for the magnificence of the Maronite Catholic church with its stately pillars, life-like statues, and high-domed ceiling with an elaborate mural supposedly depicting God staring down at us, His congregation. (To me, the man in the mural resembled our old priest, who I thought was mean and scary.) The Baptist church had no pictures or statues; its only furnishings were a pulpit, pews, and a piano.

My mother stayed in the main room, which functioned as an auditorium, while my brothers and I were led to one of the smaller rooms used for children's classes. Our teacher was the missionary, Mrs. Aynes, who was speaking in English as a Lebanese lady beside her interpreted her words into Arabic. I was fascinated. I had never met an American before and had never heard English spoken. We were taught French in school, and the French-speaking people in Lebanon resented those who spoke English, especially the British.

The missionary lady pulled a machine into the middle of the classroom (which I later learned was a slide projector), and when she turned it on, the wall before us was emblazoned with a picture of a shepherd surrounded by sheep. Through the interpreter, the missionary lady told us the picture illustrated the story of the Lord Jesus, who was our Shepherd and who loved us so much that He died on the cross in order to save us and give us eternal life. She explained that if we believed on the Lord Jesus and accepted Him as our personal Saviour, we would become His sheep, adopted into His family forever.

I believe the Lord knew this story would strike a chord in my heart because I came from a land of shepherds and sheep. My dad often drove us into the hills of Lebanon to see the many flocks of sheep led by their shepherds. We got to meet the shepherds, too, and ask questions. I was always amazed at how the shepherds were able to communicate so wonderfully with the animals and how well they knew each one. To a city boy, all the sheep looked alike, but whenever I would make an observation about a sheep that caught my eye, the shepherd never failed to give me the sheep's name and tell me everything about it.

So I loved the missionary's simple story of a shepherd's love and care for his sheep. Through it, for the first time in my life I heard that God loved me, Edgar Feghaly. I fell in love with

Him, and even as a little boy, I wanted to learn much, much more about Him.

After Sunday school, I asked my mother if we could visit the Baptist church again. She answered that if I were ready the following Sunday, she would take me with her. I could hardly wait for the week to pass so I could return to the place I had heard of the Good Shepherd.

The next Sunday, after leading us in singing a few songs and teaching us a Bible verse, the missionary once more projected a picture against the wall. This time, it was of a man standing in front of a door with one hand raised. She told us the picture represented Jesus knocking on the door of our hearts, and if we would let Him in by believing on Him, He would save us.

As a little boy, I was intrigued. I didn't know that my heart could look like a house and have a door. Furthermore, I didn't hear anybody knocking at this door. But I was also confused. Even if I were to hear knocking, I didn't know how to open the door of my heart and let Jesus in. Not quite grasping the symbolism of that story, I decided I needed to solve the mystery; I needed to look for the door. I wanted still to know more. After Sunday school, I asked my mother if I could go to the rest of the services. She initially discouraged me, thinking I wouldn't have the patience to sit through a thirty-minute sermon, but seeing my persistence, she allowed me to stay.

And so, disregarding the opposition of those around us who embraced the Catholic and Orthodox religions, my wise, courageous mother continued to take us to church. We attended the Sunday morning service, the Sunday evening service, and the Wednesday evening prayer meeting and Bible study. Eventually,

I began to understand more about the Bible and God's plan of salvation. I learned that "Saint" Mary was indeed a great woman, because, of all the women who have dwelt on Earth, God chose her to bear Jesus—but it was the Lord Jesus, not Mary, who left Heaven and came to Earth to be sacrificed for the remission of our sins. I learned that God loved me and was not only interested in my life, but wanted to have a relationship with me. He was not the vindictive God of the Catholic church, who loomed over the congregation waiting for someone to step out of line. The hopelessness I had felt about being able to do right and follow the traditions of the church slowly waned the more I attended the Baptist church and learned from the Bible.

In every Sunday school lesson and church service, the missionaries faithfully held to the Word of God and explained His plan for the salvation of mankind. And once I grasped the truth of how to be saved, the Holy Spirit began to convict my heart. One Sunday night in 1956, the missionary preached a sermon entitled, "Today Is the Day of Salvation; Tomorrow Could Be Too Late for You." It was a simple sermon but very profound, and it seemed to be aimed directly at me. The missionary told of different people who had heard the gospel and been convicted by the Holy Spirit of their need for salvation but had postponed their response to the Lord's call to their detriment. He urged us to avoid making the same mistake and to surrender to Jesus right away, before it was too late for us as well.

The message was especially meaningful because in those days our country was experiencing mild political unrest. Although civil war in Lebanon had supposedly ceased with the landing of U.S. Marines in Beirut, those opposing the continued rule of the Lebanese president periodically sent reminders of their presence by bombing various regions of the country. But as a young boy, I had yet to fully realize the danger of our situation and the implication of continuing to put off the soft call of the Lord that I had been hearing for some time. I wanted to fully surrender, but I still had doubts. What if I lost all my friends once I gave my heart to Jesus? What if I were ridiculed or further bullied and persecuted? Was salvation worth the price I'd have to pay?

These doubts were merely the lies of Satan, who Jesus called a liar and the father of lies (John 8:44). His words are poison, and his sole objective is to make a person doubt God, His salvation, and His book. What Satan neglected to mention was that any friends I might lose or any ridicule I might endure would pale in comparison to the myriad new and far better relationships awaiting me in the family of faith. But that night I listened to the doubts, and the missionary's invitation came and passed without me giving my heart to the Lord. Leaving the church after the service, I was surely the most miserable boy in Beirut.

The very next morning I was playing in my backyard when suddenly there was a loud noise and I found myself flying through the air. When I landed, I could see my mother and our neighbors pouring out of their stores and homes and rushing to me. They surrounded me, vying to hold or touch me, crying to know whether I was hurt. Shaken, I asked what had happened, and with fear in her eyes my mother replied that a bomb had just exploded and if I had been nearer to it, I would have been killed.

As I heard her words, I realized what the devil had tried to do. His plan was that I die and spend eternity in Hell, but God had intervened to spare my life. As the day went on, in my mind I replayed the words of the missionary from the night before: "If you were to die tonight, where would you spend eternity?" I knew if I had died in that explosion, I would have gone straight to Hell. By midnight I could no longer ignore the conviction of the Holy Spirit. While my parents and family were sleeping, I jumped out of bed and knelt to pray the simple prayer I had learned in Sunday school: "Lord, forgive me; I am a sinner, in Jesus' name."

A sense of overwhelming peace flooded my heart, and in that moment I finally understood the meaning of a song we'd learned in Sunday school, "The Joy of the Lord Is My Strength." Jesus had just come to live in my heart, and I was gloriously saved.

The Turning Point

My mother, brothers, and I continued to attend the Baptist church faithfully after my salvation, and my father steadfastly refused to join us. We were not surprised at this. My father was very religious, deeply entrenched in the Catholic church, and he held a position of some notoriety in our district. He was the well-respected godfather of many children on our street and throughout our entire area, but he was also feared as a mean person, known for his physical strength and willingness to fight anyone who dared challenge him. In fact, people would come from all over just to arm-wrestle him, but no one could defeat him.

My dad's tough exterior was only a cover for his constant anxiety and fears that had developed over years of struggling to survive the fallout from world wars and other political conflicts that had taken a personal toll on his life. During World War I, as a young teenager, my dad saw the Ottoman Turks rule the Middle East with an iron rod. They frequently forced men walking along the street to serve in the Turkish army and targeted for extermination those who were educated and could think independently, knowing that an illiterate and ignorant people could be controlled and mobilized to fight the Empire's wars. My grandfather managed to escape the Turkish military and go into hiding, but at great cost; my father grew up without his father, no better than an orphan. During those dark days, he lived literally from hand to mouth and while scarcely more than a boy, he had to beg from strangers to help care for his sisters.

Shortly after the British defeated the Ottoman Turks, World War II began. By then my dad was a young adult. He again experienced the paralyzing fear and anxiety brought on by foreign armies invading and fighting over their land, and he relived the terrors of death and the unknown as he watched many of his friends die of starvation and disease. By the time the Allies claimed victory and the French rule over Lebanon had ended, the wounds of war had deeply scarred my father's heart, causing him to turn more and more to his religion and devote himself to Saint Mary and the Maronite Catholic Church. But later in his life, the Lord used key incidents to show my father the ultimate emptiness of his beloved religion.

The first incident involved an announcement made one day by the Maronite Catholic Church that Saint Mary was performing a miracle in a church up in a mountain district recognized for the famous cedars of our country: a likeness painted of the Saint and hanging near the altar was shedding tears. When news of this miracle spread, tens of thousands of the church's faithful members began to flock to the mountain village to pay homage to Saint Mary. To control the crowds and provide security, the Lebanese army sent a military detachment up to the cedars of Lebanon. It was headed by a man named General Kazzi, who was a close friend of my father's. The general, an intelligent and highly educated man from a prominent family, determined to reserve his opinion about the miracle until he could observe the phenomenon for himself. He stood guard with his men inside the church and watched as one after another, people brought money, touched it to the glass framing the portrait, and then placed it as an offering in a nearby collection basket. The people interpreted the tears as Saint Mary's message to the devout that she would answer their prayers, but not everyone's prayers were answered. The general noticed that while some people who touched coins to the glass were delighted to see a tear drop from the corner of Mary's eye, others received nothing for their similar effort.

Curious about why the tears were produced at some times and not at others, General Kazzi waited until the crowds had gone, then took the portrait from the wall and removed its frame for closer inspection. He found, to his surprise, a water-soaked sponge had been strategically placed behind the portrait exactly in the area of Saint Mary's eye, and a tiny hole had been punctured through the image's tear duct. He realized that the timing of the "tears" was not random; those who did not see water when they pressed their coins to the portrait were simply not pressing hard enough against the glass to make contact with the sponge on the other side. The exposure of this scam created such a controversy that General Kazzi was punished and demoted. He later left the church and became a believer in Christ.

This incident shocked my father and undermined his devotion to the Catholic church. He began to see the church as manipulative and deceitful, which only grew clearer when he observed the priests' treatment of wealthy members of the Maronite Church. My father noticed that priests would increase their visits to rich members who were on their deathbeds and pressure them to give their inheritance to the church in order to be assured of a mansion or house (depending on the value of their estate) on a hilltop somewhere in Heaven. This practice made the church wealthier and wealthier while the families of the deceased were deprived of their rightful inheritances and driven to poverty.

Growing ever more distrustful of the Catholic church, one day my father visited the widow of one of his recently deceased relatives, a man who had spent so much of his earnings to feed his tobacco and liquor addiction that his wife was left very little to live on. My father entered the widow's home to find her in such deep conversation with a priest that neither noticed he had arrived. The priest was delivering bad news to the grieving widow: while the church had tried valiantly to push her husband into the gates of Heaven, the crowd around him also begging entrance was so great that they could not prevail. If the widow would just give more money to the church, her generous gift would strengthen their efforts, providing the exact boost needed to push her husband through the heavenly gates to his eternal rest. Just as the already poor woman was about to give the priest all the money she had, my father angrily seized the man, beat him soundly, and threw him from the house.

Considering my father's previous devotion to the Catholic church, many people questioned his decision to marry a woman who was Orthodox. It was simply unheard of for a Catholic to marry a non-Catholic. But his faith in the church and its integrity had been so shaken that he grudgingly tolerated my mother's religion instead of casting her aside as an infidel. And when she wanted to take us to church, he allowed it. He figured that his children would find the Baptist church just as boring as the Catholic mass and become fidgety and restless and that my mother would eventually give up the idea of church altogether, believing it not worth the hassle. When we headed to the Baptist church that first Sunday, my dad read his newspaper at home and awaited our return. He was surprised to see us return happy, singing the hymns we had just learned. The second week, I came home repeating John 3:16 and the beautiful story my brothers and I had heard. The more we attended the church, the more we loved it, and the more curious my father became. He could not believe there was anything about church that could cause such excitement.

After about two months, my dad could no longer control his curiosity. He told my mother that he wanted to come with us to see for himself what this place was all about. So the following Sunday, our entire family went to church. That day my dad heard that the answer was not in trusting a church for salvation, but in trusting in the Lord Jesus Christ, God the Son who came in human flesh to shed His blood for the remission of our sins so we would no longer need to fear death and Hell. He heard that Christ, the sinless and perfect sacrifice, is able to save anyone to the uttermost and once saved we are God's children and destined for eternity in Heaven. When the missionary closed the sermon with an invitation for people to come forward and give their lives to the Lord, my parents went forward together to receive Christ as their Saviour. That day, we could all feel the joy of the Spirit of God in our home. What a time of rejoicing it was!

That Sunday night after we all had read the Bible and gone to bed, my dad knelt by his bed to pray. In my room nearby, I lay in bed praying, too. As I prayed, I saw what appeared to me to be a bright florescent light coming from my dad's bedroom. I drifted off to sleep wondering what it could be. The next morning, Dad looked shaken as he greeted us. He told us he had seen a bright light as he prayed the night before and then felt a hand holding his shoulder and heard the Lord speak to his heart. He said God told him He would bless and take care of our family. I'm not sure what my father saw or heard that night, or whether it was the Lord Jesus who appeared to him or an angel from the Lord. But I do believe God confirmed his salvation and assured my father of His guidance and protection.

The salvation of my father was a major turning point for our family. Our entire family now belonged to the Lord, and He began to use us greatly. Dad became a courageous witness for Christ and an active layman, deacon, and treasurer of our church. He and the missionary pastor—who later shared that ours was the first family he'd led to Christ—grew to be as close as brothers. And a few years later, at the age of eleven, I walked forward in church and surrendered my life to serve the Lord. Through the faithfulness of a missionary to water the seeds of faith planted by God generations before I was born, these were only the beginning of the spiritual blessings that were about to flood my family.

Two

A LIGHT IN THE DARKNESS

Although I knew at a young age that God had called me to serve Him, the night I walked the aisle at the Baptist church to surrender to His will I had no idea what a life of service would involve. I just knew I wanted to tell everyone I met about the One who had changed my heart and my family. And soon, God blessed me with opportunities to do just that.

The 1950s brought the advent of tent meeting revivals in countries across the world, and through them Lebanon was introduced to evangelists like Samuel Doctorian and Maurice Hana, great preachers powerfully used of the Lord to reach many. One year, in preparation for a tent revival, our pastor gathered all the deacons and men in the church and encouraged them to bring unsaved visitors with them to the revival meetings. Then he asked for volunteers to attend preliminary prayer meetings and pray for many to be saved and to witness to people who raised a hand during the meetings to receive Christ as Saviour. He held up red ribbons, which volunteers would need to wear on their suit coat lapels as identification because at least a thousand people were expected to attend the meetings.

I was standing with my dad as the pastor spoke to the men. When he asked who would like to volunteer, I moved forward and raised my hand, expecting to receive a red ribbon. To my disappointment, he explained I was too young to participate. I turned to my father and told him I wanted a red ribbon, but he agreed with the pastor, telling me this was a task for adults, not children.

I didn't understand why I couldn't help. I knew Jesus, and I had a Bible. The only thing missing was the red ribbon all the other soulwinners had—but I knew where I could find one. Later, I went to my father's store, found a roll of red ribbon, and cut off a short length. I thrust the ribbon into my pocket, fearing it would be taken from me if I showed it.

On the first night of the revival meetings, I took the ribbon from my pocket and pinned it to my suit jacket, and I waited excitedly for the service to begin. The sermon was wonderful, and, at the preacher's invitation, many people surged down the aisle to receive Christ. As the volunteer soulwinners took people aside to go through the plan of salvation with them, I looked to see if anyone was left without an escort. Finally, I saw a boy close to my age who had come forward and was standing by his father. Joyful at the opportunity to do something for the Lord, I moved toward the boy with confidence and asked if he was saved. He didn't seem to know much about Sunday school or the Lord Jesus Christ. I pointed to my red ribbon, showed him the Bible in my hand, and explained I was one of the men responsible to lead people to Christ. I asked if he would like me to show him how to be saved, and he nodded, looking very impressed.

With as much dignity as I could muster, I took the boy aside, sat down, and began to tell him about the Lord. It suddenly occurred to me as I spoke with him that I didn't exactly know how to lead someone to Christ. I began to understand why this might be a task better suited to an adult—or at least someone with more training than I had. But I had committed myself and I had pinned on that red ribbon, so I was determined to win this boy to Christ. I knew two Scripture verses by heart, having learned them in Sunday school, so I opened my Bible to the first, Matthew 11:28, "Come unto me, all ye that labour and are heavy laden, and I will give you rest."

I told the boy that Jesus calls upon us to come unto Him, and if we come unto Him, He will in no wise cast us out (John 6:37). I asked if he would like to come to Jesus. He looked puzzled.

"Come where?" he asked. "Where is Jesus?"

I explained that Jesus is everywhere, and He loves little children and would like to save them and give them eternal life. I gave him my testimony as proof that Jesus had saved me, and then I turned in my Bible to the only other verse I knew by heart, John 3:16, "For God so loved the world, that he gave his only begotten Son, that whosoever believeth in him should not perish, but have everlasting life."

As the first verse I ever learned, John 3:16 was indelibly impressed in my memory, and I recited it as I pointed to the words on the page for the boy to follow along. When I finished,

I asked if he would like to receive Christ as his Saviour, and he nodded. I asked him to repeat the little prayer I'd prayed not that long before: "Lord, forgive me; I am a sinner, in Jesus' name." After he prayed he looked up and, at my question, assured me he had prayed from his heart.

I was thrilled. I had led someone to the Lord! I took the boy's hand and dragged him toward my dad, who was standing with a group of men from our church. I proudly presented the young convert and reported what had just happened. Moments later, as the boy made his way back to his father, my dad's gaze fell upon my red ribbon. He asked how I'd gotten it, and I told him the truth. "But Dad," I finished, eager to emphasize the most important part of the story, "I led him to Jesus!"

It was the occasion of those tent meetings that first stirred the desire within me to serve the Lord through evangelism. I saw firsthand how evangelistic meetings could impact lives long after the revival week had ended, keeping the flame of revival burning and bringing holy joy and excitement to God's people. I began to look for opportunities to share the gospel with others. When I was fourteen years old, the Lord opened a door for me to lead Sunday school when our teacher resigned. This new opportunity was not without challenges, as my English was not very good, and the Child Evangelism Sunday school curriculum we used in those days was written in English. But I taught from memory the lessons I had learned, and God abundantly blessed, compensating for my lack of knowledge. Within a very short time, my English had improved so significantly that I was able to interpret sermons for our missionary pastor. And God continued providing opportunities for me to serve Him as I grew older. My brothers and I became active in youth meetings and summer camps, and I began to play piano and lead singing in church services. I often went with the national pastor on visitation and witnessed to a number of people. Later, I was able to assist as an interpreter for other missionaries and American pastors who visited Lebanon.

As I grew older, my love for the Lord and my passion for serving Him only deepened, and God began to open doors to tell others about Him not only through church ministries, but in the secular world as well. In 1967, I was of age to begin preparing for college, but though Lebanon's economy was growing, higher education was only within reach for the very wealthy. My father's business had begun to suffer. While the income from the store was adequate for our day-to-day living, I had to find work in order to help my father provide for our family and to earn money for my continued education.

Banking was a major industry in Lebanon, and my elder brother had obtained employment with a British bank. So I set about to follow his example. The Lord directed me to a job with the Beirut branch of the First National Bank of Chicago, where I was expected to begin as a lowly office clerk and learn all I could in hopes of being promoted.

I worked hard at the bank, and my coworkers soon found I was quite different than they were. Determined not to compromise my faith, I did not smoke, drink, or curse as many of them did. Furthermore, I made sure everyone knew I was a follower of the Lord Jesus Christ. I witnessed to people whenever the Lord presented an opportunity.

My testimony and desire to please God did not sit well with my coworkers, who often made fun of me with subtle innuendos or outright mocked my faith. It did not take long to realize there were people in the world who, through jealousy, unhappiness, or pride, would spend enormous time and effort plotting harm, suffering, or even destruction for others in an endless quest to become popular. Nonetheless, I endeavored to be gracious and kind to my coworkers. Sometimes this would lead to their genuinely curious questions about my faith during coffee breaks. On these occasions it was a joy to take my time explaining to them the grace of God and His redemption. However, while everyone I worked with—including my manager—eventually asked me a question about the Bible, most intended only to mock me and my Saviour.

Despite being later promoted to a higher position with the bank, I was still mistreated and mocked. After a while I began to be discouraged, thinking things would never change. I poured out my heart to the Lord in utter frustration, asking why He allowed these people to continually ridicule my faith and give me so much grief no matter how faithful I was to show kindness to them.

Let it not be said the Lord does not hear the cry of His children! His very specific answer came through two incidents that happened in the bank shortly after. The first took place one day as I was working. A man who had often ridiculed me approached the counter where I sat and leaned across it, his chin in his hands, looking distinctly embarrassed. After a little prodding, he asked if I would do him a favor. He was running short on cash and needed to borrow money. He promised to repay me when he received his salary. I was quite surprised that a man who would harass me would feel so free to make such a request, but I realized this was an opportunity to show him the love of Christ. I gave him the money, which greatly increased his embarrassment. He thanked me and walked a few feet away, then stopped and backtracked as if he'd had another thought. He humbly apologized for his unruly behavior toward me. Then he told me something truly unexpected: although my coworkers mocked me, they secretly had great respect for me. They knew I was honest and one of the few trustworthy people at the bank.

What an answer this was from God! I was encouraged by the assurance that the world can see when we stand for Christ. That day I walked home from work rejoicing and thanking the Lord for revealing this truth and encouraging me.

Not long after, the second answer to prayer came through a conversation about my working hours. My job often required me to work overtime, but because I was not required to work Sundays, I typically put in my overtime hours during the week so I could attend church on Sunday. One day, however, a Lebanese manager came to me and told me he needed me to be at the bank on Sunday. I respectfully told him why I was unavailable, but he became angry and shouted that every other employee worked on Sundays and I had better do the same.

The noise drew the attention of his superior, the bank's American general manager, who asked what had happened. When he learned I did not want to work on Sundays because that was the day I worshipped the Lord, he told the other manager that I could not be forced to work and the Lebanese manager should find another employee for Sunday overtime.

This incident opened a new door for me to witness to several other managers (some of them Muslim and Druze Muslim) and explain how my faith in Christ motivated me in my work and my daily life. I knew that being a follower of Christ in my community and taking a stand for Him in my workplace could come at a very high price, such as losing my job. But I had learned from the Scripture about Daniel, who took a stand for God as a young man and saw His blessing even in the midst of trials and testing. And just like God's repeated deliverances of His servant Daniel in pagan Babylon, He took care of me.

As I grew in my Christian walk, I began to govern my life according to principles drawn from the words of Christ found in the Bible:

> *And he said to them all, If any man will come after me, let him deny himself, and take up his cross daily, and follow me.*—**Luke 9:23**

> *Neither do men light a candle, and put it under a bushel, but on a candlestick; and it giveth light unto all that are in the house. Let your light so shine before men, that they may see your good works, and glorify your Father which is in heaven.*—**Matthew 5:15–16**

> *Ye are the salt of the earth: but if the salt have lost his savour, wherewith shall it be salted? it is thenceforth good for nothing, but to be cast out, and to be trodden under foot of men.*—**Matthew 5:13**

Therefore all things whatsoever ye would that men should do to you, do ye even so to them: for this is the law and the prophets.—**Matthew 7:12**

To me, carrying the cross daily had to do with my identity with Christ. Christ was not popular in His day; He reminded the disciples that He was hated by the world (John 15:18). So I determined not to worry about what the world thought but to be identified with my Saviour. And because I knew those around me were watching me and I realized my life could either be salt and light to show the glory of my Saviour or it could bring reproach to His name, I determined to have a good testimony before the world. Finally, I wanted people to love me and treat me with respect, so I determined never to return evil for evil, but to treat others with kindness and forgiveness.

Of course, I was not perfect. But though I sometimes stumbled, I strove to let these principles characterize my life. I truly believe that my willingness to be a light for God and share His love with others through service and testimony was made possible because the Lord instilled His love in my heart and the desire to tell others about it at a very tender age. The blessing of the Lord on the life of an eager young boy with a borrowed red ribbon sparked spiritual decisions and life changes that made all the difference for eternity.

Three

THE STORMS OF WAR

My childhood in Lebanon during the 1950s was very simple. My family lived in a three-bedroom apartment on the ground floor of a building in West Beirut, in a relatively peaceful community where Christians, Muslims, and Jews lived side by side. We didn't have much money; we lived off whatever revenue my father's store brought in each day, with my mother often making family meals from vegetables and a small bit of meat. Sunday dinners were special because Mom bought a chicken to stuff with rice and made her special chicken soup and garlic dip. The meal would simmer while we were at church and fill our home with delicious smells.

Like most of the folks in our area, we did not have a television, so we entertained ourselves by visiting our friends and relatives, swimming in the Mediterranean Sea, or watching the people and events taking place in Al Hamra Street—a main commercial street often described as the Champs-Élysées or Manhattan of Lebanon. The American University of Beirut could be found there, which became more interesting to my siblings and me as we grew older and became more aware of how our people cherished education.

Of course, the highlight of every year was Christmas Day. Early Christmas morning, we would pile onto my father's bed, and he would read the story of Christmas, pray, and then distribute our much-anticipated gifts. We would each receive two gifts and one Lebanese lira (equivalent to about seventy-five U.S. cents), and sometimes other relatives gave us an additional lira. With our money burning holes in our pockets, on Christmas afternoon we would walk down to the public gardens and rent tricycles and then bicycles for fifty piasters (there are one hundred piasters to a lira) an hour. We had great fun racing through the beautiful gardens and flower-surrounded trails with other children from the area.

Our area was called Wadi Abu-Jamil, well known for its Jewish population and influence. The Jewish people of Beirut were kind, friendly, and industrious, and my father purchased many commodities for his convenience store from Jewish merchants. During Jewish holidays, we often joined them to taste some of the special kosher foods they ate. In those days, there were no major political struggles among Muslims, Christians, and Jews in my district. But that was all about to change.

War Breaks Out

The beginning of the end of our seemingly idyllic life was signaled by Egyptian president Abdel Nasser's mobilization of the Middle

East against America. Egypt and the United States had been allies at least in word since 1954, when America sided with Egypt against Israel, Britain, and France's invasion of Egypt and occupation of the Suez Canal. But when the U.S. refused to build the Aswan Dam for Egypt, citing safety reasons, Abdel Nasser allied himself to the Soviet Union, America's enemy, who agreed to build the dam and provide arms to the Egyptian army and air force. Nasser not only rejected the United States, but he also poisoned the Middle East against American ally, Israel, by declaring Israel was an enemy of Arabs. The majority of Middle East nations were ruled by socialistic dictatorships that gave absolute power to the military and secret police. Because Israel was not a dictatorship, these totalitarian governments insisted Israel's existence among them was illegal. The atmosphere of the Middle East became increasingly politically toxic as Arabs began to resent the West in its support of Israel. Arab leaders were certain Israel could and should be annihilated, so they armed themselves for war, purchasing war planes and weapons from the Soviet Union to amass a formidable force.

As a democracy ruled by minorities who could still think for themselves and were not swayed by Egypt's rhetoric, Lebanon was the only exception to this growing animosity and tension. But by the mid-1960s, as communism gained traction in the Middle East and pressures mounted for Jewish people, life in Lebanon became much less simple. We had been accustomed to paying little attention to the political climate around us; after all, we'd heard Arab leaders threaten Israel in the past to divert attention from their own economic problems. But something about this time was different. Daily, newspaper headlines trumpeted frightening statistics—huge numbers of military weapons stockpiled by Arab nations, increasing numbers of battle-ready soldiers—that seemed designed to erode Israel's confidence in its own military resources. Each day's headlines concluded that, should the Arabs decide to go to war, Israel's destruction would be inevitable. Arab leaders even openly discussed what to do with any surviving Jews after the war was over, and some politicians suggested they be sent back to Europe or thrown into the sea to drown or drift as the waves pleased.

Although we carefully read the papers daily, we still did not believe war was possible. And then, early on the morning of June 6, 1967, just a few days before my high school graduation, we were awakened by tremendous noise on the streets—and my hopes for graduation were dashed.

As a Lebanese teenager growing up in a poor family, I had looked forward to my high school graduation. I had done well in high school and eagerly anticipated the class celebrations and field days (in which I fully expected to win medals). But more than anything else in the world, I wanted to march in my graduation ceremony.

As we looked out our windows the morning of June 6, however, to our utter amazement, we saw rank on rank of tanks and army trucks moving along the street accompanied by hundreds of military personnel. We rushed to turn on the radio to find out that the Arab countries had declared war on Israel, and this time, they weren't bluffing.

During the early days of the war, we remained glued to the radio, anxiously awaiting the latest developments from Beirut, Damascus, or Cairo. At first, the announcers confidently reported that the Arabs had won a decisive victory against Israel, and their armies were marching toward Tel Aviv, Israel's capital city. We heard breaking news of great numbers of Israeli tanks destroyed and Israeli soldiers killed, which caused jubilation among Lebanese Muslims; their demonstrators filled the capital and other cities, denouncing Israel and America and shouting, "Today, we get rid of Saturday; tomorrow, we get rid of Sunday!" which meant, "First, we will get rid of Israel, and later we will get rid of the Christians." This sent a wave of fear among many Christians, who were terrified the Muslims might make those threats an immediate reality. We realized our only hope was in God's intervention on our behalf, and we fervently prayed He would protect us.

As the war progressed, we began to wonder just how deeply the Arab soldiers had penetrated into Israel. If there were no Israeli military resistance, as the Arab media claimed, why had the Arab armies not yet reached Tel Aviv? After all, Israel was not a large country. When we tuned in to BBC London and Voice of America, we were shocked to learn it was the Arab armies, not the Israeli Army, that was retreating in defeat because the Israeli Air Force had completely destroyed the Egyptian and Syrian Air Force from the very first hours of battle. Israel postponed its official declaration of victory for six days to give Arab soldiers time to surrender their weapons and return to their capitals; Israel did not have the prison capacity to hold so many prisoners of war.

The Arabic defeat sent a tremendous shock wave throughout the Middle East. Muslim demonstrators again poured into the streets, this time to express their rage against their leaders, who could not believe they had been so handily defeated. They tried to excuse their loss by claiming the United States had deployed Marines to the shores of Israel to help its ally. These points were stressed so powerfully that many ordinary Arab citizens began to consider America the enemy of the Arab world and scream for the death of both America and Israel.

We Christians who lived in Lebanon began to wonder if Bible prophecy included anything pertinent about the turmoil surrounding our region, and true believers developed a great interest in studying prophecy. One of the main chapters we frequently studied was Isaiah 19, which many Christians felt referred to Abdel-Nasser, a charismatic leader who, through his speeches, could rouse nations to war.

> *And the Egyptians will I give over into the hand of a cruel lord; and a fierce king shall rule over them, saith the Lord, the Lord of hosts.*—Isaiah 19:4

> *In that day shall Egypt be like unto women: and it shall be afraid and fear because of the shaking of the hand of the Lord of hosts, which he shaketh over it. And the land of Judah shall be a terror unto Egypt, every one that maketh mention thereof shall be afraid in himself, because of the counsel of the Lord of hosts, which he hath determined against it.*—Isaiah 19:16–17

We found another intriguing prophecy in the gospel of Luke: "And they shall fall by the edge of the sword, and shall be led away captive into all nations: and Jerusalem shall be trodden down of the Gentiles, until the times of the Gentiles be fulfilled" (Luke 21:24).

One of the results of the Arab-Israeli War in 1967 was the Israeli forces taking East Jerusalem from the Jordanian army, which protected the Arab section of the city. Lebanese Christians saw Israel's decisive victory and its uniting of a previously divided Jerusalem as a fulfillment of the prophecy of Isaiah 19.

Whether or not Isaiah 19 refers to the Israeli-Arab War, Egypt was soundly humiliated and Abdul Nasser, its fierce dictator president, resigned from office and saw his power and influence fade. But what added salt to the wound of the Arab nations' loss was the taking and complete occupation of Jerusalem by what they called "Zionists," who in their minds were different from ordinary Jews. Arabs saw Zionists as the wicked element within Israel whose agenda was to destroy Arabic nations and occupy the Middle East "from the River of Egypt unto the Great River, the River of Euphrates" as spoken of in Genesis 15:18. In response, Arabs determined to follow Hitler's example from two decades earlier and try to annihilate the entire nation of Israel, a focus that completely destabilized the Middle East for years to follow.

As for Lebanon, the Arab-Israeli War changed my beloved, formerly innocent homeland forever—seemingly overnight. Politics became dominant, tensions rose high, and it became clear that the days in which Muslims, Christians, and Jews could live together in safety and peace were over. It deeply grieved me to see many of the missionaries and Jewish neighbors we loved leave Lebanon forever. In all likelihood, we painfully realized, we would never see them again.

Yet, God was present in these troubling times, and we remained faithful to serve Him. I continued teaching Sunday school and telling Muslim and Catholic children about Jesus, and I continued to see many accept Him as Saviour. In years to come, we were blessed to hear stories about a few others who we had witnessed to, but did not personally see, receive salvation. In later years, a Jewish friend who remained in Lebanon told my dad that our neighbor had accepted Christ as her Saviour in response to my father's witnessing to her on several occasions. Her family disowned her, and though I do not think I will ever meet her again on Earth, I know I will see this dear lady again in Heaven.

Among my favorite stories is one I was not told until more than thirty years later. The family of a Muslim boy who attended our Sunday school moved with his family to East Lebanon and settled in an area called the Beqaa Valley. He was unable to attend church for many years, as there were none in the area, but one day when he was an adult with his own children, he was visited by a passing evangelist who stopped to witness to him. After hearing the gospel once more, he gladly received Christ as his Saviour. He later visited our church in Beirut and told me how the Word of God, planted in his heart through our Sunday school so many years before, had born wonderful fruit.

Black September

After their surprising defeat in 1967, Arabic nations—some of whom became known as the Palestinian Liberation Organization (PLO)—realized they would need to pour resources into strengthening their military if they ever hoped to be able to win a war against Israel. Their goal won them widespread popularity, so that the PLO soon outstripped the leaders of surrounding Arab nations. Muslims all over the world declared their determination to support and encourage their military efforts, and vast sums of money began flowing into the PLO's coffers. With increased support, the PLO's confidence and influence burgeoned, and Yasser Arafat, the Sunni Muslim leader and chairman of the PLO, became so powerful that Arab leaders practically fell over each other to please him, fearing their own people would turn against them if they did not.

Jordan, a country ruled by King Hussein bin Talal, was home to the largest population of Palestinians in the Middle East, after many sought refuge there following the birth of Israel in 1948. These refugees later applied for and received Jordanian citizenship and eventually outnumbered native Jordanians. In this manner, the PLO grew strong in Jordan without much government opposition. Unlike the Arab armies, PLO commandos could cross the borders of Southern Lebanon, Jordan, and Egypt to attack Israel. The propaganda justifying these attacks taught that the Palestinians were killing the evil Zionist infidels and reminded audiences that destroying Jews was considered *halal* (lawful, legitimate, permissible). Those Palestinians who died in the attacks received a royal funeral and were hailed as heroes and martyrs.

The PLO grew so strong that it virtually became its own state within Jordan, and its presence was felt everywhere in the Middle East. Several smaller leftist organizations operated under its umbrella, including the Popular Front for the Liberation of

Palestine (PFLP)—which received worldwide attention in 1970 when it hijacked four commercial planes and landed them in Jordan, released the passengers, and then blew up the planes. These acts were hailed as heroic by Arabic PLO supporters, but they shocked the rest of the world and caused a great deal of embarrassment to the Jordanian government, whose authority and power were called into question.

Tensions had already risen between Jordan and the PLO as the PLO asserted its authority over Palestinians in the country. Its members paraded through the streets of Jordan in a show of power intended to humiliate the Jordanian army. And PLO supporters had increasingly been calling for the overthrow of Jordan's King Hussein for his traitorous pro-West stance and lackluster effort during the 1967 Arab-Israeli war. But it was the PFLP hijacking and the accompanying world reaction that prompted King Hussein to begin a campaign to expel the PLO from Jordan.

King Hussein informed the Israeli government of his plan to engage the PLO in battle, and Israel promised its assistance should any Arab country interfere on the side of the PLO. Though outnumbered, the Jordanian Army fought the PLO in the streets of Amman, in cities all over Jordan, and in Palestinian camps. The Syrian government soon came to the PLO's aid with two hundred tanks, broke through the much weaker Jordanian defenses in a major offensive, and forced Jordan to retreat. Without additional forces to stop Syria and fearing a division of the Iraqi Army would seize opportunity during Jordan's weakness to join the PLO against him, King Hussein nearly sought aid from America and Israel. But victory over Syria came through Jordan's own Air Force with a series of aerial attacks that severely disrupted the invading army's incursion. Badly beaten and fearing intervention by the superior Israeli Air Force if it retaliated against Jordan, Syria pulled back its troops and ignominiously retreated from the conflict in defeat.

Over the next days the rest of the world watched in amazement as the battle between the PLO and the Jordanian Bedouin Army progressed, and Jordan gained ground by quietly locating PLO snipers hiding inside homes and launching mortar bombs through residential windows to kill them. On September 25, 1970, just weeks after the conflict had begun, a cease-fire was declared with Jordan, the decisive victor of what the PLO later referred to as "Black September." Tens of thousands of Palestinian military members and civilians had been killed, Palestinian camps where weapons caches had been stored were leveled, and Palestinian leadership had been decimated. Less than a year later, King Hussein succeeded in driving the PLO from Jordan completely, leaving the group to recover and rebuild from its headquarters in a new country—Lebanon.

Just as it had done in Jordan, the PLO set about establishing its own Palestinian state in Lebanon, arming and training young Palestinian men in refugee camps-turned-army bases. And just as it had in Jordan, the influx of fighters into these Palestinian camps and the steadily growing influence of the PLO inflamed tensions with the Lebanese government. As tensions heightened over the next few years, Lebanon became a time bomb on the brink of explosion.

Four

A SPIRITUAL DOOR OPENS

Although nations around us were in turmoil, Lebanon's experience in the years immediately following the first Arab-Israeli War was quite different. Lebanon had not joined the fight against Israel, and it rapidly became both a political battlefield and a refuge for those who were kicked out of their countries or found themselves searching for jobs. But also drawn to our country during this time were Middle Eastern leaders looking to invest or hide money through Lebanon's sophisticated banking system rather than travel to Switzerland or other European countries; millions of tourists who came to enjoy Lebanon's natural beauty and moderate weather; and Arab and European students attracted by the American University of Beirut and Jesuit University, which were considered easily as rigorous as the best universities in Europe and America. Buoyed by the revival of major construction, boosts in tourism, and its new status as a transit center for Middle Eastern land and sea imports, Lebanon saw unprecedented prosperity practically overnight.

But the affluence that characterized 1968 through 1974 was not to last. The Lebanese people were lulled by our sudden success into a false sense of security. We thought nothing terrible could ever happen to us like what had happened to our neighbors. And so we failed to see the activity within the Palestinian camps under PLO leadership, the efforts of leftist and Communist Palestinian organizations to build up armies with the goal of full mobilization, or the smuggling of weapons into Palestinian camps under the benevolent protection of the United Nations. We were blind to both the rising political tension and frequent demonstrations in surrounding countries and the increasing political instability of our own country. Dark clouds were forming on the horizon, threatening the security of Israel and Lebanon, but we missed it all.

Another Arab-Israeli War

Egypt's Abdul Nasser died in 1970, but his goal of destroying Israel lived on with Egypt's new president, Anwar Sadat. Believing he would be able to defeat Israel in a single battle, Sadat began to build his army and enlisted the aid of twenty thousand Russian advisors to train the Egyptian armed forces for battle. Other Arab leaders joined in the effort, turning to the Soviet Union for support in the form of Soviet-made SAM and SCUD Anti-Aircraft Missiles.

Around midnight on October 7, as Israel celebrated Yom Kippur not expecting an attack from the Arabs (who were also engaged in religious observance of their fasting month of Ramadan), the Egyptian and Syrian armies launched a coordinated offensive. In order to cross Israel's fortified first line of defense, the Egyptians had imported powerful water cannons from Germany and blasted through high sandy hills to create openings large enough for their troops and machinery. Additional troops and tanks crossed the Suez Canal across bridges built expressly to surprise the Israeli defense and dominate its front lines. Within hours, Egyptian commandos and infantry had employed anti-tank missiles to decimate two-thirds of an Israeli front line defense that had been previously considered invincible.

Under cover of the anti-aircraft missiles, the Egyptians moved into the Sinai Desert to further press their advantage, but Israeli forces stopped the incursion. Two days later, Israel had mobilized its armies and counter attacked both the Syrian and Egyptian armies. After forcing back the advancing Syrian army, causing them to suffer heavy losses, Israel advanced within twenty miles of the Syrian capital city of Damascus. In Egypt, the success of the Suez Canal attack was eclipsed by the Israeli army's infiltration of Egyptian forces. On October 23, Israel crossed the Suez Canal and encircled Egypt's Third Division. By that time, the world was intervening to stop the war, which had already proven devastating to both sides. Israel lost 800 tanks and 100 aircraft, and 2,800 soldiers were killed while another 8,200 were wounded. Arab losses were greater; 1,850 tanks and 450 aircraft had been destroyed, and 28,000 soldiers had been either killed or injured.

Although much of the world watched and weighed in on the second Arab-Israeli War (also called the Yom Kippur Arab-Israeli War), once more Lebanon refused to become involved. The turmoil and political coups outside of Lebanon mattered little to us. And while Lebanon's refusal to war against Israel further infuriated the Arabs, hastening the outbreak of civil war in Lebanon, we did not care that our inaction might displease Arab leaders. We just enjoyed our oasis, our happy corner of the world, living for the pleasures of the moment and little worrying what agony the future might have in store.

The gospel of Luke records Jesus giving His disciples this warning: "And as it was in the days of Noe, so shall it be also in the days of the Son of man. They did eat, they drank, they married wives, they were given in marriage, until the day that Noe entered into the ark, and the flood came, and destroyed them all" (Luke 17:26–27).

These verses accurately describe life in Lebanon during this time. The people were so busy enjoying the material things of life that, although they were shocked and grieved for Israel, they did not dream Lebanon's day was coming as well.

Moment of Opportunity

I believe God allowed this time of relative peace and prosperity for Lebanon in the midst of world turmoil because the influx of millions of Arab tourists from all over the Middle East created an unprecedented opportunity to bring the gospel of Jesus Christ to lost souls. The years between 1967 and 1975 saw tens of thousands of witnessing opportunities. Many Muslims and non-Muslims received Bibles. Ships carrying all kinds of literature and Christian books were able to dock at ports with thousands of patrons able to board to purchase Bibles and Christian literature. The spiritual door to the Middle East was Lebanon, and we Christians took advantage of it.

Although the missionaries who left Lebanon in the turbulence of the first Arab-Israeli War never returned, a new wave of missionaries soon moved into the region. They were followed by Christian organizations such as Campus Crusade for Christ, the Navigators, InterVarsity Christian Fellowship, Operation Mobilization, and other similar groups. The missionaries, Christian groups, and our church in Lebanon worked together for the sake of the gospel, and we saw tremendous blessing. Bibles and tracts were shipped into the country in massive numbers. We took them into areas where Arab tourists resided, gave them copies of the New Testament, and witnessed to them about the Lord. In this manner, hundreds of thousands of people all over Lebanon from all denominations heard the gospel.

We were not alone in the work. Young people from many other churches in Lebanon joined forces with others who came from the West to evangelize the lost. In 1974, Dr. Bob Jones, Jr., Chancellor of Bob Jones University, visited Lebanon, hosted by the Bible Baptist Church of West Beirut. Ours was just one of several churches where Dr. Jones was scheduled to speak. He did so during one of our Sunday evening services. People came from all over the city to hear him, and as was customary at that time when any American pastor visited our church, I was asked to interpret.

What was especially memorable about that service was what happened afterward. As we stood talking for a moment, Dr. Jones invited me to come to Bob Jones University in South Carolina to continue my education. At the time, I had a good job and was ready to settle down and enjoy life in Lebanon, but I thanked him anyway. I took the application he offered and completed it as a courtesy. I delivered the application to Dr. Jones at his hotel, but I had no real thoughts of going to Bob Jones University. I just did not see how it could be a realistic option for me. I had no thought that the God who knows the future was preparing me for a far greater task than any He had yet given me: a life in ministry that I could not possibly have envisioned.

One of my favorite verses is in Ecclesiastes: "Remember now thy Creator in the days of thy youth, while the evil days come not, nor the years draw nigh, when thou shalt say, I have no pleasure in them" (Ecclesiastes 12:1).

This was the theme of my ministry among the young people of Beirut. I was determined to serve my Lord while I could, despite all the distractions and Lebanon's material attraction. And so, by the grace of God, while most of the young people in my country were partying, drinking alcohol, and smoking, I was determined to use my time telling people about the Saviour. These years, and particularly 1974, were exciting because I was privileged to share Christ without fear. Though my faith was resented and opposed by many, by God's grace, I was undeterred and ready to defend it.

The Power of the Gospel

While sinners coming to repentance is always cause for great rejoicing in Heaven, such was not the case on Earth, and particularly in Lebanon in those days. Some of the stories I heard from people who gave their lives to Christ were, frankly, shocking.

One story I heard directly was from a young man named Zach, who worked in the bank under my supervision. Zach was of Egyptian-Palestinian background. Before his salvation, he had been a Sunni Muslim and a member of the PLO who had participated in the Palestinian resistance against Israel. One day as he was walking the streets of Beirut, a man gave him a gospel tract and witnessed to him. As a result, Zach received Christ as his Saviour, resigned from the PLO, and gave up violence against Israel. Eager to share his faith, Zach began to visit mosques in Beirut specifically to witness to those who attended prayers there. He used his considerable knowledge of the Koran to engage imams in public debate and ask questions about the Islamic religion that religious leaders could not answer.

One day, Muslim extremists sent two men to Zach's small apartment to execute him by slitting his throat—a common punishment on apostates. Zach opened his door to these men and instantly realized they intended to kill him. The PLO had trained him in martial arts, and he held a black belt in karate, so he backed into his living room and as the men drew their daggers and rushed into the apartment, Zach landed a powerful kick in the first assailant's middle. The man flew through the air, struck his head on the corner of the dining room table, and died instantly. When the second assassin saw his friend was dead, he dropped his dagger and fled. But the danger for Zach was not over. Shortly after, he left Muslim-dominated West Beirut to take refuge in the safer area of East Beirut.

Another account came to me through the owner of a building in the suburb of Haddath that housed a church where I ministered. The church was overseen by the missionary that had led me to Christ, and every Tuesday I assisted him as interpreter for the mid-week service. One day, the building owner told me about a man who needed a job and asked for my help. Apparently, the man would sit idly at home while his wife supported them through house cleaning jobs. Then he would take her money and waste it on alcohol and movie theaters. When she could not find work, he would beat her. Once he became so angry at her that he attempted to stab her. Desperate to survive, she ran from their home, and when he chased her, she threw a stone that hit him in the head and injured him enough to end the altercation temporarily. After hearing about this man, I was not eager to help, but I told the building owner to invite him to attend the service that night.

The man came to the service Tuesday night and listened to the sermon. As I stood at the door greeting people after the service, he shook my hand and asked me to pray with him. I went through the plan of salvation and prayed with him. The next week as I visited a family in the neighborhood, the head of the family asked, "What did you guys do to Waji?" Waji, I soon discovered, was the man who had come to church looking for a job but found Jesus instead. After the service, Waji returned home to his wife, kissed her, and in tears apologized for all the harm he had done. He promised from then on that he would be a good husband and would find work to provide for his family.

Waji kept his promise to his wife and became a faithful man and a powerful testimony of God's love and salvation. Eventually, he found a job as a building caretaker for a Lebanese judge. Though the judge was a highly educated secular man, Waji in his simplicity was able to witness effectively to him. This judge would often call Waji to his home to ask him questions about the Lord.

Sometimes I had opportunity to join with my father in witnessing to those who visited his convenience store. My father was always looking for opportunities to witness to his customers. Through his testimony many received the good news of the gospel and became his loyal friends. One day as I visited him at the store, I met one of his friends, George, who was also a prominent leader of the Communist Party of Lebanon. This man was an atheist who loved his party with an almost religious fervor. I knew this was a God-given opportunity to witness. As we sat drinking coffee, George told me he thought I was very intelligent, but I was wasting my youth following the teachings of Jesus rather than the greater teachings of Karl Marx. He offered to help me go to the Soviet Union and enroll in the best Russian university. He promised that although I was from a poor family, the Communist Party would help me to become a lawyer, doctor, architect, or anything that I wanted. All I had to do was forget about Christianity, and I could take advantage of this once-in-a-lifetime opportunity.

I looked at this man who had just made a luxurious offer by the world's standards and told him I already had a Master in

Jesus and would rather stay poor and pay for my own education than to have a scholarship and go to Communist Russia. Angry at my rejection, George began to rant against biblical teachings as fantasies invented by Jews to enslave the nations. I listened for a few moments, but my spirit was stirred as I realized how the devil had deceived him into thinking he had all the answers. There he sat praising his beloved Communism and its supposedly peace-loving heroes such as Stalin and Lenin who had ruthlessly murdered their own people and allies while mocking the One who had come in love to redeem the world from such evil.

I decided to confront George that moment. I took a coin from my pocket, flipped it in the air, then caught it and covered it with my hand before asking him whether it was heads or tails. Thinking I was refusing to take him seriously, he repeated his offer and told me again it was the chance of a lifetime. I too was serious. I repeated: "Heads or tails?" and told him he had a 50 percent chance of being correct.

Clearly disgusted, he spat out, "Heads!" but when I asked how he could be sure, he admitted he could not know. He was confused now, with no idea what I was attempting to illustrate. I told him the odds on that coin flip were similar to the odds he was right about his beliefs. He believed there was no God, no Heaven or Hell, and no salvation. If he were right and I were wrong, I lost nothing because God's Word teaches us to love and respect others, work hard, and live honestly—which makes us happy people. But if he were wrong and I were right, he would lose everything and be destined to suffer eternally in Hell.

I gently but firmly gave the good news of the gospel to George, telling him Jesus was his sacrifice, He is greater than Marx or Stalin, and He is the only one who saves and gives eternal life. George did not accept salvation that day, and we never again discussed politics or Communism, but from then on he showed me much respect whenever we met. Sadly, shortly after the Lebanese War began, George was killed and robbed by two of his Communist friends who had discovered he was carrying a sum of money with him. I have no doubt that today George remembers our conversation and regrets refusing the opportunity God gave him to repent and believe.

One of my favorite stories is of a man I met a few weeks after I witnessed to George. One day my dad called me at work to tell me there was a man in his store he wanted me to meet. When I arrived there later that day, a well-dressed and smiling man was waiting for me. Dad introduced him as Mr. Azar, a born-again believer in Christ whose children went to my high school and were my friends. I was glad to receive Mr. Azar as a friend and talk with him about the Lord, but not long into our conversation, something in my spirit told me that though this man knew a lot about the Bible, he had not truly accepted Christ as his personal Saviour. Something was hindering him— something I was unable to put a finger on.

Before Mr. Azar left my father's store, he asked for the address of our church and said he would like to attend regularly. He lived just twenty minutes from the church, so I volunteered to walk with him on Sunday morning. As we walked, I questioned him more about his faith, his work, and his life. He began to speak about good and bad angels that influence people's decisions and shared that he could communicate with them. He also claimed to have received messages from God, delivered by the prophet Isaiah and the Apostle John. I quickly realized Mr. Azar was not a Christian, but a spiritist.

Christians believe on the authority of the Word of God and that the Holy Spirit alone guides us to the truth by means of the written Word of God. We believe Satan is pure evil, and all the angels who fell from Heaven and are identified as demons in the Bible are Satan's minions who now do his bidding. Those holy angels who did not rebel when Lucifer (Satan) did are recorded in Scripture as God's messengers. Apart from these two groups of spirit beings, there are no "good" or "bad" spirits. Spiritists believe one should seek the good spirits in order to fight off the bad spirits (a concept that is diametrically opposed to Scripture), failing to realize that it is not "good" spirits with whom they communicate, but demons. And while Satan and his demons may try to entice others with bits of truth, that truth is always poisoned, twisted, and designed to distract and move people away from God.

Just a week before meeting Mr. Azar I had read a book entitled *I Talked with the Spirits* in which the author, Victor Ernest, wrote of his parents' involvement in spiritism and described many things that went on inside a house where spiritists met to conduct séances and communicate with the spirit world. Mr. Azar confirmed the things I had read as he told me of being invited by a friend to a spiritist meeting and being amazed at the spirits' ability to move things around during the séance. His curiosity piqued, he began attending the meetings regularly, and the more he attended, the more attached he became. Though he suspected the spirit manifestations were not genuine, he could not resist continuing to attend. When his children ridiculed his new beliefs, he invited them to experience a meeting for themselves, and they were quickly hooked, just as their foolish father had been.

Using the information I had learned from the book on spiritism, I was able to convince Mr. Azar that I knew a lot about the cult. I explained the truth from God's Word and invited him to receive Christ as his personal Saviour because only Jesus could set him free. After some soul-searching, Mr. Azar prayed to receive Christ and "passed from death unto life" (1 John 3:14). The joy of the Lord quickly became apparent in his life. He developed a genuine love for reading the Bible, and I later heard he had begun to witness to his children about Jesus as well. I thanked the Lord for allowing that book to come to my attention at just the right moment so this man could be set free from bondage to demons by the power of our Lord and Saviour.

One last story also reminded me in those days of the power of God. This incident involved a mysterious magician who lived a few blocks from our home. Reports abounded of the stunning feats performed by this man who was so powerful that many were afraid of him. A Lebanese pastor heard of the magician and wisely took two of his deacons along to witness to him. At their knock, the magician's servant led the trio into the guest room to await the magician, but the man would not come out to meet his visitors. The servant returned to tell them his master knew why they were in his house and that he would not see them or speak with them about salvation because he had made an agreement with the powers of darkness. He believed if he spoke with them, the Evil One would kill him. What irony: this man who had frightened so many was himself scared of three simple men who worshipped the Lord Jesus!

Strength for the Days Ahead

These are just a few of the highlights of 1974, when it seemed the Lord was giving people around us an abundant opportunity to hear of Calvary. God broke the chains of spiritists, communists, and Muslims proving His power to be greater than anything in this world. Truly, this was the year I learned that "in all these things we are more than conquerors through him that loved us" (Romans 8:37) and "greater is he that is in you, than he that is in the world" (1 John 4:4). The Lord Jesus provided us with the full armor of God with which to attack the devil and his kingdom and provided us a defense against his fiery darts (Ephesians 6:13–18).

As the year came to a close, we prepared to celebrate Christmas and New Year's Eve as always. We had no hint that the spiritual door that had been opened to us was a blessing that would strengthen us for the days to come when Lebanon would head toward an upheaval so tremendous that most of our lives would be forever changed. Believers gathered at our home on Christmas Eve to sing, praise the Lord, and enjoy fellowship over cake, fruit, tea, and coffee. This would be our final such celebration in Beirut, for very soon everything we had would be gone, and many of our precious friends would scatter in fear for their lives.

Five

EVERYTHING CHANGES

April in Lebanon marks the return of spring with bright flowers bursting into bloom, vibrant green grass poking through the soil, and warm breezes from the Mediterranean Sea. The sharp cold, wet, and mud of Beirut's winter gives way to beautiful sunrises from behind majestic eastern mountains, colorful sunsets over the Mediterranean, and a change of mood in the people from somber endurance to noticeable jollity. This is how I had experienced springtime ever since I could remember. But the spring of 1975 brought no joy, only foreboding as the newspapers brought tidings of an intensifying political situation across our homeland.

It seemed we heard almost daily of anti-government demonstrations taking place, and although our media recorded the military buildup with plenty of photographs, we did not need those to show us the Lebanese military was everywhere; we saw its jeeps with anti-aircraft machine guns posted throughout the city and the surrounding countryside. But many other political parties were building their own militias, the largest of which was the Phalangist Militia, a Maronite Christian organization that recognized the grave danger represented by the PLO in Lebanon and thus urged the government to deport PLO militants to Syria. But the Lebanese government in those days was weak.

To make matters worse, Lebanese Muslims supported the PLO and soon agitated for the creation of an Islamic state with a Muslim rather than a Maronite Christian president presiding over the country. The Lebanese Army was composed of about 25,000 soldiers, 40 percent of whom were Muslim and sided with the PLO, and there was legitimate concern that attempting to deport the PLO would split the army and lead to civil war with an entirely unknown outcome. Realizing the army would not defend Lebanon, the Phalangists began to build their own army. Meanwhile, socialist Arabic countries continued to arm the Sunni Muslim militias and the PLO while Israel and Jordan trained the Christian militias. With such an abundance of weapons and ammunition flooding a tense country, Lebanon soon became a ticking time bomb waiting to explode into war.

Sunday, April 13, seemed like any other Sunday. We awoke and prepared for church as usual, and then I assisted a missionary in a suburb of Beirut while my brothers went to our home church in West Beirut. Both services went well, and afterward my parents, brothers, and I sat down to an enjoyable lunch complete with fellowship and discussion of God's blessings in our lives. After lunch and a nap, my mother prepared our traditional afternoon Turkish coffee and Nescafé. We spent a leisurely hour together before getting dressed to head to church for the evening youth meeting and worship service. My father believed Sunday was a day best spent meditating on God's Word and the sermons we had heard, not listening to the news or reading the paper. Thus, we had little idea that anything was amiss in the world outside our home.

But that evening, my elder brother had stayed behind for a short time as the rest of us headed to church as usual. And in the middle of the service, as I interpreted for the missionary who was deep in his sermon, I saw my brother rush into the church, his face full of anxiety. He motioned for our Lebanese pastor and my dad to meet him outside. After a couple of minutes, the Lebanese pastor returned and announced the service was over and everyone needed to return to their homes immediately.

Raising his voice above the din as everyone began speaking at once, my brother told us the President of the Phalangists had been attending mass at the Maronite Catholic church of the Ain Al Ramani area, a noted Christian stronghold, when gunmen in a car had opened fire on the church with a machine gun. Fearing for the life of their president, militias in the area were all on alert, and blockades had been set up along the roads to check the identity of every car passing by the Maronite church. A short time later, a bus had passed the church and refused to obey militia orders to stop. The bus was carrying Palestinians attending a political rally, but the militiamen concluded they were assassins and opened fire on the bus, killing everyone on board. The PLO interpreted the act as a premeditated attack on its people, and it was not long before fear spread that the PLO would exact revenge by attacking areas inhabited by Lebanese Christians. We were certain Lebanon was heading to a civil war, and we were terrified. If street fighting were to begin, there would be no safety for anyone.

We did the only thing believers can do in such a situation: we prayed for God's protection upon us. Later that evening, when no attack had materialized, Dad suggested we all go to bed, pray, and try to sleep. But about midnight we awoke terrified at the deafening noise of exploding mortar shells as bombs began falling in our areas. Between explosions we could hear the cries of our neighbors as they too began to realize we were under attack. We were confused and particularly defenseless, as our home was on the top floor of our building. Not one of our rooms was safe or offered shelter from the blasts, so in sheer panic, we sought shelter in a neighbor's house and waited out the attack for the next two hours. When the shelling finally stopped, we wearily returned home and once more attempted to sleep, but with heavy hearts, for we knew this was the beginning of a new and desperate chapter for Lebanon. War had come to our country.

Warning Signs and Close Calls

Over the next days, our streets filled with well-armed militia units. Although we were first warned not to move around too much, after a week, the situation settled down enough for us to return to work, which brought a small semblance of normalcy back to our lives. But danger always lurked about the community. While Beirut remained relatively calm during the day, no one dared walk out at night or go beyond his area even in the day time.

Meanwhile, as in the wider world around us groups that opposed Israel joined the war in Lebanon, militias began actively recruiting or forcing young people to join their ranks. One day I received a call from a young man in our church named Abrahim. Upon his salvation, he had turned from his Druze Muslim background and begun carefully hiding the Word of God in his heart in order to be an effective witness and defender of the Bible and his faith. Not long after Abrahim was saved, baptized, and had joined the church, his sisters and brothers began to attend, and several of them also received the Lord as Saviour. Over a period of years, we developed a close friendship with Abrahim's family, and he became not only my partner in soulwinning, but a very dear friend.

Abrahim called to deliver a message from his brother, who had joined the socialist militia that exercised control over the area where Abrahim lived and where our church was located. His brother, who knew me well, had warned Abrahim that my brothers and I were on a blacklist, wanted by the militias—not because we were criminals, but because we were known for our Christian witness. To them, I was responsible for attempting to convert Abrahim and others in the area, so I was a threat. Abrahim's brother urged me through Abrahim to stay away from my church.

I was deeply grieved at the thought that I would no longer be able to minister in my church, but I knew I should follow this advice. Determined to still serve the Lord, we began to seek out other churches in safer areas. We traveled to southern Beirut to a church in Haddath, where we were able to reach more young people. Before long, we started a fellowship meeting to bring young people from different churches and reach new areas with the gospel. We met in the home of a professor living in the area. I preached, my brother led the singing, and the Lord blessed by leading many young people to receive salvation and commit their lives to Him.

The Bible teaches us that we gain strength from the joy of the Lord (Nehemiah 8:10) and that He is our refuge and shelter in times of trouble (Psalm 46:1). In Him we find safety. We experienced the reality of this truth as God brought great peace in the middle of the turmoil churning around us. The ministry the Lord gave us in Haddath and the spiritual fruit borne in southern Beirut more than compensated for the inability to attend our home church.

Needing to leave my church was not the only warning sign that the war in Lebanon would exact a personal toll on my life. In the fall of 1975, there were more attacks in Christian villages in northern, southern, and eastern Lebanon. In September, pro-Syrian forces attacked the Monastery Dar Ashash in northern Lebanon and killed three priests. In October, the same forces assaulted a village called Telabbas, killing fifteen people and injuring many others. Villages inhabited by Christian minorities were occupied by Muslim militias supported by Syrians and the PLO, and the people were either attacked outright or aggressively pressured to vacate their homes.

Imprisoned in Freedom

Lebanon's instability slowly forced Beirut businesses to close down. In October, the owner of the company I worked for sent a memo stating that the employees who were missing many work days would soon be in danger of being laid off. We were also informed that the president was seeking opportunities to relocate the company to Cairo. We all desperately needed the income provided by our jobs. No one in Lebanon was hiring at the time, and my parents' business was no longer generating much income because people were living in fear and curtailing their spending. Most Americans and foreigners had left Lebanon, schools were closing down, and people did not stray too far from their homes.

By December of 1975, most of the employees of my company had left their jobs. The handful of us who were left continued working because we considered our need of income worth the risk of traveling through the city. But on Saturday, December 6, 1975, we heard a rumor that made businesses around us panic, close up shop, and go home early: a battle was coming that would last far longer than anything we had previously experienced. I gathered our employees to talk about a strategy for our next steps. We agreed we would stay put and continue working in the relative safety of our building. However, we needed food for our "encampment," and since there were not many grocery stores nearby, I volunteered to go home and purchase food from our family store.

I took a taxi home, and by the time I bought the needed staples and meat, the streets were totally empty, with hardly any taxis to be seen anywhere. No one I asked about the emptying streets knew what was going on, but it was clear the situation was serious. I had to get the food back to my coworkers because they were relying on me, and I knew if I did not return they would not dare venture out. Our butcher, a Sunni Muslim, offered to take me back to work because it was on his way home. I agreed, assuming that he had a car but was surprised to find that he had a motorcycle. I climbed on behind him, carrying two large bags filled with food.

Instead of taking me directly to my work, the butcher told me he had an errand to run, and of course, I had no choice but to go along. I began to feel uneasy when he drove us through heavily populated Islamic areas where I would fear to go even in times of peace, areas known as the heart of the Islamic resistance. He stopped in front of a place where militias were known to assemble, asked me to wait outside, and entered as if looking for someone. He must not have been successful because he soon returned only to drag me to another Islamic militia base looking for some relatives or acquaintances. To my relief, the second place was completely vacant, but by now, I was growing more suspicious. We were far out of the way that the butcher knew I needed to go.

He told me he had yet another errand to run, after which he would take me to work. Realizing I could not trust this man, I could only answer an almost shaky, "Fine," and pray for the Lord's protection. He drove to a gas station a couple of miles from my company, but although the station was open, again, no one was there. The butcher looked frustrated and a bit confused. On the way to the station I had become more convinced that my life might be in danger and had been thinking of ways to get away from this man. Here, I saw my opportunity. I got off the motorcycle, politely apologized and thanked him for his help, and told him I would walk the rest of the way. I prayed and hoped he would not follow me and find out where I worked.

After a long walk I finally reached the office, and when my coworkers heard of my adventure, they confirmed my fear that the butcher had meant to harm me. They explained that four members of the rightist Phalangist party had been found dead in an abandoned car near the power plant in Christian-dominated East Beirut. Because one of those murdered was the son of Joseph Saad, a party military leader, Saad sought revenge. His militias targeted Muslims through stopping people at checkpoints, and as a result many Muslim lives were lost. In return the Muslims began to retaliate by kidnapping and murdering anyone who was non-Muslim. Because I was a regular customer and the butcher knew me well, he likely had not wanted to kill me himself. Instead, he was looking to deliver me to someone else who would do the job. But the Lord was with me; He protected me and delivered me out of danger. That night we all slept in the company offices, and as I closed my eyes, I rejoiced and thanked God for my safety, realizing He was not yet finished with me.

Around midnight one of the men awoke to noise on the highway across from our building. Peeking out of the window, he saw obvious movement of columns of militias. The next morning, he told me we had a problem: that highway seemed to be the supply line of weapons and ammunition for the leftist Muslim militias. This news truly frightened me because the Muslims had no way to distinguish between Maronite Catholic militias and born-again Christians. If they found a group of young people hiding in a building, they would naturally think we were spies and would not hesitate to kill us. I called an urgent meeting and instructed everyone they were not to leave the offices under any circumstances until the situation calmed down. We could not even trust the man who managed the building, as he was a Druze Muslim and the Druze militias were also mobilizing to fight against the Rightist militias. We were trapped in the middle of enemy territory.

We prayed earnestly for deliverance, and on Monday, the Lord again provided miraculous protection. Our company had hired an advisor, a Greek Orthodox businessman who served as a consultant to our president and Board. I discovered later that he was also on the board of the PLO and personally knew Yasser Arafat. This man's offices were on the same side of the building and not far from us, so I called him and told him we were in the office working and that we were afraid. I asked his advice on what we should do.

He confirmed that we were indeed in danger and that we needed to take extreme precaution so that the militias would not discover our presence. He told me once the situation calmed down he would send some of his men to take us to our homes. He warned me to lock the doors and not to open them for anyone, and he gave me a phone number to call if a stranger knocked. He asked me to go to the balcony to identify some secret PLO intelligence members, and I discovered our building's garbage collector and shoeshine man were actually PLO officers. Thanks to our new friend, these men would now join others in the vicinity to keep an eye on us.

I thanked the Lord for our advisor because, although he was not a born-again Christian and did not go to church, he was aware of the testimonies of those who followed the Lord Jesus Christ. He knew we were not violent and posed no danger, and I was sure the Lord moved in his heart to help us. A few days later, he called back to tell me the situation was calmer and we should prepare ourselves to be escorted to our homes.

As I was packing, I realized this might be the last time I would see this company, as I was again heading into the unknown.

A few hours later, a black limousine and two jeeps filled with heavily-armed militia men arrived in front of our building to take us home. Nervously, we ran out and climbed into the limousine next to the PLO officer, who assured us we were quite safe. The car drove us all the way to the line of demarcation and stopped in front of the Lebanese Museum, where the officer explained they had taken us as far as they could and from there we were to walk to East Beirut. As we climbed out of the car, he asked us to tell our families what he had done for us. We earnestly thanked him, and then the car and jeeps drove away and we made the rest of the journey into East Beirut, the Christian stronghold, on foot.

As I walked, I thanked the Lord—the one truly responsible for our safety. I could not help but remember how God sent ravens to care for the prophet Elijah when he fled to Beersheba and how God moved the heart of the King of Persia to authorize the rebuilding of the walls of Jerusalem and the temple in the days of Ezra and Nehemiah. My heart was thrilled at the realization that the very same God who had performed such mighty miracles for His Old Testament servants had before our eyes moved the Muslim PLO militias to rescue us even as they were fighting against the Christian right-wing militia.

I also realized that I had left my office building that day for the last time, and, although I was physically walking home, I was headed into the unknown. The only thing left for me in Lebanon was serving the Lord. Between December of 1975 and March of 1976, my younger brother and I sang and shared the Word of God in different local churches, intensified our efforts in the youth meetings, and spent much time in visitation and soulwinning. Though we were persecuted by many, we did not care. God provided great courage as we publicly spoke about the Saviour. Many of the people we visited would ask about the end of days, and I would explain what the Bible says. All this made me forget that I no longer had income. The company had not paid our salaries for several months, and my financial resources were dwindling.

A Difficult Decision

By the spring of 1976, the city had calmed a bit; militias from both sides were taking their position but without shooting at each other. One morning in March, my family was going about our usual routine and conversing casually about what might happen next when my father abruptly changed the subject and suggested we venture into the mountains to visit my sister. It seemed an oddly spontaneous idea, but what was more interesting was the way the family responded. Normally I might have plied my father with questions, but I asked nothing. My elder brother, who might have argued it was not a good time for a trip, calmly arose and grabbed his car keys without hesitation.

And my mother, who had been washing dishes, simply left them in the sink and declared she was ready to go.

Almost surreally, we found ourselves in the car, driving quickly through the narrow streets of Beirut and up into the mountains. My brother wished he had brought a couple of suits with him. My mother wished she had changed her kitchen dress and worn something nicer. I wished I had brought some books to read. But when we reached my sister's home in the mountains, we realized our spontaneous trip had been yet another instance of God's miraculous protection of our family. The uneasy calm that had settled around Beirut had broken. Not much earlier, the Muslim militias, the PLO, and the Lebanese Arab armies had formed an alliance with the leftist militias of the Lebanese National Movement and as one force they prepared to invade the strip of Beirut occupied by the right-wing militias. One short hour after we left our home, the battle began.

Much of the action was centered around the local Holiday Inn, which was destroyed in the fighting. After several days, the right-wing forces pulled out of the Holiday Inn and market area, leaving civilians behind. Those who stayed home and could not leave were massacred by Muslim forces, resulting in the first major bloody battle of the war. Had God not intervened, we would have been numbered among the casualties. How marvelous was the Lord's deliverance!

While at my sister's house, an old neighbor whose children were in the militia and who had pulled out of the area called me with awful news. During the battle, several mortars had landed on our home, demolishing it, and a rocket-propelled grenade had destroyed my father's car. Worse, Dad's store had been looted and burned. He had literally lost everything he owned.

My father had worked diligently all his life to maintain his home, and as a man who deeply loved the Lord, he made sure it was always open for believers in Christ to come and enjoy fellowship. My father's car was not only for entertainment or business. Even unfamiliar with the American church tradition of bus ministry, my dad used his car like a bus to go around, pick up people, and take them to church. His store was also used for the Lord: he kept Turkish coffee brewing constantly, and when a customer came in to purchase something, my dad would invite him to have coffee. If he accepted the invitation, Dad would pull his Bible from the drawer and witness to the customer over coffee. When in his later life Dad's eyesight became too poor to clearly read the Scripture, he posted verses around the store and would point them out to the customer, beginning with Romans 3:23 and ending with John 3:16, providing a clear outline of the gospel and mankind's need of a Saviour.

My heart was broken for my dad, who I knew would never be able to recoup any of the losses at his age. I called my older brother into one of the bedrooms to formulate a plan for how to tell my father the news. As we talked together, Dad opened the door and asked us what had happened. I had no choice but to tell him simply as I had heard it. As I finished the litany of bad news, I tried to think of something to comfort him. My mind went blank, and I stood helpless and speechless. My father moved toward us and put his arms around our shoulders. He told us quietly that the night before, he had prayed and surrendered everything he had to the Lord. He had told God that if it were His will, He could take the house, the car, the store, and anything else my dad had because it all belonged to God anyway. All he asked was that God spare his children, and because we were all alive and well, Dad told us he was grateful to the Lord for answering his prayer. (My dad never recovered any of his losses. He spent the rest of his life witnessing and telling people about the Lord Jesus until 1980 when he went to be with the Saviour he loved.)

We waited out the end of the battle in the mountains. When it finally ended, with no home to return to, we moved to live temporarily in my grandmother's home. Though we had little, we continued witnessing and serving the Lord.

Although the battle that took our home was over, the war still raged in Lebanon. Not long afterward, my younger brother—who had by this time married and had a baby with his wife—encountered some difficulty of his own. One day a bullet pierced the window of his master bedroom, terrifying my sister-in-law. She visited her pastor, understandably discouraged, and asked him why God would allow this to happen. The pastor could only answer that for the believer all things work together for good (Romans 8:28), and that in war, dangerous things should be expected. But my brother and sister-in-law determined Lebanon was no longer safe for their family, and they decided to move to France.

This was a real blow to me because my brother and I had been a great team as we supported each other in serving the Lord. I couldn't help but question how this could possibly be God's plan. Though I did not realize it at the time, the Lord was beginning to teach me a great lesson in faith. Like the eagle that seems to treat her eaglets cruelly by thrusting them from the nest, God allows us to go through trials and tribulation for our benefit. But there was a deeper lesson as well. In the middle of the night, shortly after my brother left Lebanon, a stray mortar crashed through my brother's master bedroom window, landing on the bed and destroying the entire room. It became clear to me then that the Lord sometimes allows drastic things to happen to protect His children from something worse. God foresaw the incident and allowed my brother, sister-in-law, and their daughter to leave the country for their own safety.

The year 1976 was not even halfway over, but to those of us who lived through the war in our homeland, those days seemed unending. The born-again Christians among us could not help but wonder what the Bible had to say about the war in Lebanon. We diligently searched the Scripture and were intrigued by what we found in the Old Testament:

> Open thy doors, O Lebanon, that the fire may devour thy cedars.—**Zechariah 11:1**

> For thus saith the Lord unto the king's house of Judah; Thou art Gilead unto me, and the head of Lebanon: yet surely I will make thee a wilderness, and cities which are not inhabited. And I will prepare destroyers against thee, every one with his weapons: and they shall cut down thy choice cedars, and cast them into the fire. —**Jeremiah 22:6–7**

It certainly seemed Lebanon was being devoured by fire and destroyed by enemies on all sides. As a result of the war, most of the truly good Lebanese leaders and many innocent people were killed by militia bombs and army attackers from outside Lebanon (such as the Muslim PLO, Muslim mercenaries, and pro-Syrian forces). Many Christian-inhabited towns and urban areas were demolished, and many Lebanese were displaced. On top of that, due to the war, my family had lost our home and everything in it, my brother—my partner in ministry—had taken his family and left Lebanon, and I had lost my job and could not find another. Over the course of many months, I began to realize things could not go on as they had been. With no means of supporting myself, I was only helping to faster consume my parents' already limited resources rather than contribute to our survival. With no sign of things changing in the near future, I was forced to admit that the time to leave Lebanon, the only home I'd ever known, had come.

Six

STEPS OF FAITH

June of 1976 marked a turning point in my life. I had finally accepted that my only option was to leave Lebanon, but the idea was intensely painful for me, and the future was full of unanswered questions. If I left, would I ever see my family again? Would my church ministries survive?

Yet, as painful and uncertain as leaving was, I determined to go. I heard that the owner of my old company had successfully opened a branch in Cairo, so I decided to move to Egypt and continue working for the business. As I bid my parents farewell, I tried my best not to show any emotion. I assured them I would come back to visit, and I sincerely hoped the situation in Lebanon would quickly improve so we could be reunited permanently. But I knew I was not guaranteed another meeting with them and that this might well be the last time I would see my family.

Guided by God

With just enough money to make the trip to Cairo, I left Lebanon for Syria, then continued to Egypt, believing this would be the last leg of my journey for at least a few years while I settled into my job. But upon my arrival, my hopes were shattered when the company president told me he had been unable to legally register the company and thus could not hire me. He offered to compensate me on a temporary basis if I finished the balance sheet and the financial report, but he could do nothing more.

With my plan now ruined, I had nowhere else to turn. I could not return to Lebanon because the airport was closed, and I could not stay in Egypt because I would soon run out of money. That night I went to bed disappointed and confused, and for the first time in my life, I felt I had lost all vision and objective. I had no direction. It was as though life had simply stopped around me. In desperation, I prayed to the Lord, crying out for guidance. I knew I was His child and could trust that nothing would happen in my life apart from His will and His plan, but at that moment, I could not see what He had in mind for me. I earnestly prayed He would show me the way. Then, I slept.

The next day I was in the Cairo office finalizing the company's financial statement and balance sheet, but by the middle of the day, I began to sense a puzzling urge to leave Cairo and go to Alexandria. Now, it had long been a principle of mine to finish what I started, but this urge was so strong that I put aside my work, left the office, packed my suitcase, and headed to the train station. I told the company president I would finish the financial statement when I returned from Alexandria, and when he asked the reason behind my spontaneous trip, I told him I did not know it but would find out when I arrived.

Once in Alexandria, I booked a hotel room and then decided to go for a walk. As I explored the city, I tried to take in everything around me, all the while praying God would show me why I had been led to a city where I knew no one. I was still walking and praying when I looked up to see a pastor friend of mine named Dr. Victor Sadaka. After we recovered from our mutual shock at seeing each other, Dr. Sadaka explained he had also just arrived and was on his way to the seaport but had decided to take a walk before sailing to the Muslim-controlled area of Lebanon. Even more shocking was the reason he intended to travel to Lebanon. He was traveling with a message for me from Bob Jones University. The University had accepted my application and wanted me to contact them immediately.

As he spoke, I was reminded of the scripture in Proverbs that tells us, "As cold waters to a thirsty soul, so is good news from a far country" (Proverbs 25:25). I began to realize why God led me to Alexandria. Had I not obeyed, I would not have met Dr. Sadaka and his journey to Lebanon would have been fruitless. Further, I would have missed the now-clear direction God was showing me for my life. This was the sign, the word from the Lord I had prayed for in Cairo, revealed in God's perfect timing and through His miraculous planning.

I returned to Cairo, finished my financial report, received my compensation, and headed to Europe. I passed through Austria, Switzerland, and then continued on to France with a joyful heart, for I had something wonderful to look forward to.

God had shown me yet again that He would never leave me nor forsake me. With the writer of Hebrews, I could "boldly say, the Lord is my helper" (Hebrews 13:6).

A European Witness

My time in Europe was full of new experiences. As I was in my early twenties and this was my first time living completely independently, this could easily have been a season that damaged my testimony for the Lord. But thanks to the wise counsel of my father, I was prepared against the temptations of alcohol, drugs, or promiscuity that commonly beset unsuspecting and immature young men.

Time and bitter experiences taught my father precious lessons, many of which he shared with us after his salvation. He warned us that Satan sets seemingly appealing snares for young people and, like a spider, traps them in his web. He told us we did not even have to taste alcohol or smoke a cigarette to experience their destructive effects; we simply needed to observe the lives of others around us. He would remind us that in the biblical account of the Good Samaritan (Luke 10:25–37), the Jewish man on his way to Jericho was caught unawares by thieves who took everything he had and then left him for dead—and he warned that Satan does the same to unwary people. Then he would remind us of the adulterous woman of Proverbs 7 and warn us of the dangers of yielding to the lusts of the flesh.

As I arrived in France, my dad's warnings echoed in my mind. I determined to be like Daniel, who "purposed in his heart that he would not defile himself" (Daniel 1:8). I would not be lured by Satan into temptation and ruin, but would keep myself pure before the Lord. I truly believe it was for this reason that I was able to witness to many people in Europe and see God's power in miraculous ways.

One highlight of my time in Europe took place when I was invited by a former coworker to visit him at his aunt's house in Paris, where he had fled to escape the violence in Lebanon. I had not been in the home long before I learned two things about my coworker's aunt: she spent almost all her money on fortune tellers, as did many French people at the time, and she was plagued by nightmares every night. Although the two facts seemed unrelated to this lady, it became clear to me that the fortune teller, a Muslim man from Morocco, had introduced demons into her home. When my coworker and I returned to her home one day to find the fortune teller there, I immediately seized the opportunity to witness to them both.

As I silently prayed, claiming the blood of Christ, the fortune teller became disturbed, but I continued warning them of hell and demons, and I increasingly sensed the presence of the Holy Spirit. The poor woman told me she consulted the fortune teller because she was afraid of the future. I opened my Bible and showed her the future is held by Jehovah and that the devil may promise peace but he is a liar and the father of liars. I told her the fortune teller was lying to her and wanted to destroy her life.

She looked doubtfully from me to her nephew, who was also a Christian. She wanted to know how she could be sure God exists and could help her. I told her if she would simply place her faith in Christ, God would reveal Himself to her, free her from her nightmares, restore her marriage, and give her His lasting peace about the future. Tearful and still unsure, she asked how she could know He was powerful enough to save her. I told her that her nephew and I would both pray that night for her restful sleep. She promised that if she had no nightmares, she would believe we were telling her the truth about our God.

That night, for the first time in many years, this lady slept the peaceful sleep of a child. On waking the next day, she proclaimed that we indeed had the Spirit of God with us. My friend and I rejoiced to see the power of God through prayer to bring victory over the forces of darkness.

The College Years

Living in France relieved a lot of the tension in my life that had been rising through the war and instability of Lebanon. It was a much-needed respite from danger and uncertainty that prepared me for the next stage in my life and in my service to the Lord. It seemed every day, with every person to whom I was given opportunity to witness, I realized more fully the meaning of Paul's words when he urged Timothy to gladly take up the cause of Christ: "Who hath saved us, and called us with an holy calling, not according to our works, but according to his own purpose and grace, which was given us in Christ Jesus before the world began" (2 Timothy 1:9).

Although I had been fearful and confused about my future, the Lord had a plan for me and was directing my steps all along. He had allowed me to experience difficulties and dangers to prepare me for what He had in store. In France, I learned to follow the Lord and entrust my future to Him. Like an unfinished painting, the Almighty Artist's beautiful design for my life was slowly emerging.

Part of His design became clearer the day God placed Dr. Sadaka in my path in Alexandria. With his message in my mind, I called Bob Jones University not long after I arrived in France and discovered that I had indeed already been accepted as a student. I needed only to pay for one semester's tuition and expenses, and the university would issue me the student immigration visa required to study in the United States. To my amazement, the money I needed to pay for tuition and to secure a plane ticket was the exact amount I had in my possession. Praising God, I made plans to come to America.

The university was far different from anything I had known in Lebanon or Europe. I was older than most of the other students, but was soon able to find ways to serve the Lord without competing with them. I started an off-campus fellowship for international students who were finding it awkward to blend into campus life. Each foreign student was assigned a "campus parent" who was either a faculty or staff member of the university, but often these students would long for deeper connections with students with whom they had more in common. The idea behind the fellowship was to gather foreign students in Christian homes around the city so they could build friendships and pray for one another. Every month a student would be asked to talk about his country and its spiritual and material needs and another student would bring a challenge from the Word of God. Afterward, we would all pray for that country and for each other. As a special and unique treat at every gathering, students would prepare national dishes from their homelands to share with the group.

Our international fellowship was such a blessing, especially since many students who were considering the mission field would attend. Frequently, we would invite our professors and campus parents to join us, and we even invited Dr. Bob Jones, Jr., a world traveler who was well acquainted with most mission fields, including Lebanon. It was not long before the international fellowship drew the attention of the university, and we were invited to host these fellowships on campus so that we might include more students.

Another opportunity to serve the Lord at Bob Jones University came through Dr. Grace Collins, a professor of Linguistics who I would assist at times. Dr. Collins invited me and some other Middle Eastern students to watch a movie dubbed in Arabic on the life of the Apostle Paul. Our discussion following the movie centered on the need for an outreach to Arab residents of Greenville, South Carolina. Stirred to do what I could to help, I began investigating the possibility of starting such an outreach with the professor's help. We visited numerous Arab families and found that many of them favored the idea of starting a church, so Dr. Collins helped us secure a hall at Southside Baptist Church, one of the larger churches in the city. There we met every Sunday afternoon, and, to the glory of God, we saw people saved during this time, many of whom were from Palestine and Lebanon. Before long, the outreach meeting grew into a solid ministry that continues to this day.

UNEXPECTED OPPORTUNITIES I was born in Beirut, Lebanon, in 1949 and accepted Christ as my Saviour in 1956. Since the tent revival services shortly after my salvation and when I had my first opportunity to lead a soul to Christ, the Lord has given me opportunities to serve Him in places and capacities that I could not have dreamed.

GROWING UP IN LEBANON Above: My family (I am next to my father) standing in front of the store front church the missionaries rented in 1956—the year I got saved | **Top Right:** A tent for revival meetings in Beirut, like the one where I led my first soul to Christ at eight years old | **Bottom Right:** Sunday dinner in our home with the missionaries

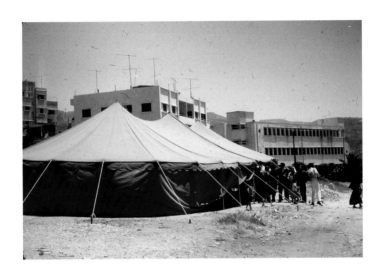

GOSPEL INFLUENCES **Above:** Mr. and Mrs. Clyde Agnes were the missionaries who led me to Christ. | **Top Right:** My grandmother (at front right) was led to Christ by a missionary lady who came to her town on the back of a donkey in the 1890s. | **Bottom Right:** My grandmother singing a song the missionary taught her—"Jesus Loves Me"

BEFORE THE WAR
Top Left: My two brothers, Robert and Raymond, Dad, Mom, and I | **Bottom Left:** My father's convenience store before it was destroyed. | **Top Right:** Interpreting for missionary, Mrs. Dwight Billingsly | **Bottom Right:** The view from the Billingsly's apartment overlooking the city of Beirut and the Mediterranean Sea before the war

A WAR-TORN CITY Top Left: During the war, we had to keep a supply of candles and kerosene to survive the long electricity outages. | **Bottom Left:** The battle in Beirut that we watched from our home in the mountains. | **Top Right:** A checkpoint in Lebanon during the war | **Bottom Right:** My father's store after it was destroyed in Beirut's first major battle (pre-war picture on previous page)

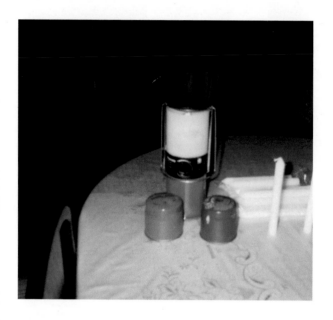

FURLOUGH
Above: Our first deputation | **Right:** Pictured with Bob Jones Jr. the year I graduated from Bob Jones University in 1980

FIRST TERM, 1985
Left: Due to the war, the airport was not accessible. The only way to Lebanon was by boat. | **Bottom:** Our view of Beirut as we entered Port Junieh

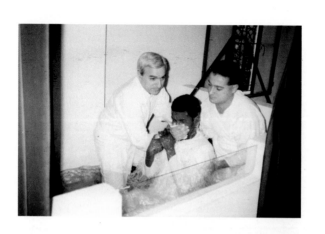

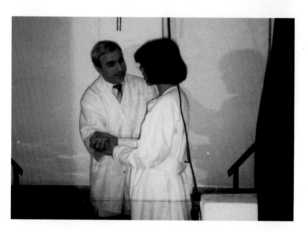

LIFE IN LEBANON **Above:** Standing by a destroyed tank after a battle in Beirut
Top Left and Middle Left: The first baptisms in our newly-established church in 1985
Bottom Left: Our family celebrating Christmas in Lebanon

FAMILY LIFE
Top Left: Our family celebrating Christmas on furlough **Bottom Left:** With Mitchell and Julie in 1990 | **Right:** Rosann and Mitchell on a camel | **Bottom Right:** In 1990 when we returned from our furlough, boat transport was still the only way to enter Lebanon.

MIDDLE EAST **Above:** The ordination of the man who took my place as pastor of the Bible Baptist Church of Beirut | **Top Right:** Mitchell and Julie, in African outfits at our church in Haddath, Lebanon, in the early 1990s | **Bottom Right:** Baptizing by night in Syria

AFRICA **Above:** A graduation of our Bible institute held in Ghana. | **Top Right:** I was able to preach to 5,000 people in Red Sea State, Sudan, and 3,000 people came forward for salvation. | **Middle Right:** Dr. Larry Clayton, Pastor Jim Alter, and I ordaining four men to the ministry. | **Bottom Right:** People getting baptized in Togo around Easter, 1999.

SUDAN Above: Visiting the governor of Sudan's Red Sea State with Pastor Craig Holmes of Alabama and pastors from Sudan and Egypt. **| Top Right:** My partner in the Moro Nation in Sudan, Pastor Mahjob, was a former stone worshiper. His children told me that he was poisoned by Muslim extremists. **| Bottom Right:** A typical response to an invitation for salvation in Khartoum, Sudan.

BAGHDAD
Above: The pastors who participated in the dedication of the New Testament Baptist Church in Baghdad. | **Right:** Pastor Maher and I baptizing the former high ranking Iraqi general, whom I led to Christ in 2004. He was later gunned down in his home by Muslim extremists.

SERVING IN BAGHDAD
Left: Danny Whetstone and I pictured with American soldiers in Baghdad. | **Bottom:** Emerging from the plane that spiraled down into Baghdad onto the tarmac at the Saddam International Airport, occupied at the time by United States forces

FORWARD FROM HERE Above: I continue to serve across the Middle East in church planting and training national pastors. I am pictured above preaching the dedication of the New Testament Baptist Church in Juba, South Sudan. All across the Middle East, God is opening hearts and working in ways many American Christians never hear about. Please pray for dear Christians around the world who are often persecuted for their faith to remain faithful to the Lord and fruitful in their witness. | **Below:** Additionally, I have many opportunities to encourage churches in the States regarding missions and what God is doing among Muslims in the Middle East. Here is a picture at a missions conference at Lancaster Baptist Church in California. Pastor Paul Chappell, and his wife, Terrie, are dear friends and prayer partners in our ministry. We thank the Lord for the many friends and prayer partners He has given to us around the world.

A New Ministry Partner

Coming to the United States to attend Bob Jones University was a blessing to me in many ways, as God provided me with a fabulous Bible education and many opportunities and connections with which I could better serve Him. One of the greatest connections God brought into my life during these years was established with a wonderful young lady who later became my wife.

I had always believed it is the Lord who brings a man and woman together, and I was confident He would help me find the right woman in His time. Little did I know He would literally place her in my path and have her reach out to me! One day near the end of the school semester, I posted a flyer on a university bulletin board to advertise the sale of a history textbook I no longer needed. Just one day after posting the flyer, I received a call from an interested young lady named Rosann, and we arranged to meet in the university snack shop to complete the transaction. I was surprised when we met to realize that although Rosann and I were not acquainted, I had seen her before and we actually shared several classes. This girl was beautiful, and there was just something about her that caught my attention. Somehow in my heart, I immediately felt this was the girl God had prepared for me.

Shortly afterward, we started dating and attending university activities together. The longer we dated, the more sure I became that I wanted to marry Rosann, so I began to tell her about Lebanon and the war, and I introduced her to my Lebanese friends who also attended the university. At that time, Lebanon was again being featured in daily news reports for another war that was raging in its streets and costing many lives. If Rosann were going to be my life partner in ministry, I needed to be very sure she understood my heart for my country and that she realized, if God should open the way for us to return to serve Him there, Lebanon would be the most unusual, difficult, and dangerous mission field imaginable—yet, it was for this reason that we could more effectively minister to the people, pointing them to the Lord Jesus Christ, the Hope of the nations. While many missionaries leave a country during times of great danger and unrest, these are times when people are most vulnerable and desperately in need of the guidance, hope, and peace offered by the Lord.

Over time, Rosann started becoming involved in the ministries in which I served, even volunteering to pick up folks for the Arabic service at Southside Baptist Church. This willingness to serve complimented two of Rosann's other most endearing personality traits: her spirit of contentment and her thankful heart and attitude. As time went by, I realized Rosann would be content to serve the Lord wherever He placed her, even in the dangerous mission field of Lebanon. As we served together and grew closer, our relationship became living proof of the fact that when God brings two people together, there is perfect harmony.

In 1980, Rosann and I graduated from college, and on November 6, 1982, we were married in the historic Niagara Frontier Bible Church in Lewiston, New York. Everywhere the leaves wore all the magnificent fall colors and, lending their beauty, made the wedding all the more romantic and memorable.

That evening, in the hotel where we began our honeymoon, we both deeply felt the need to rededicate our lives to the Lord as a married couple, so the first thing we did was to kneel and pray together. We poured out our hearts to Him and committed ourselves to service as missionaries to Lebanon as soon as He might reveal His timing and provision.

The Call to Return Home

Now that the Lord had blessed me with a family, returning to Lebanon during such a turbulent time was riskier than ever, and I knew we would have to completely trust in the Lord's protection and help. So after the honeymoon, Rosann and I moved to Toronto, where I worked as a corporate financial comptroller, and Rosann worked as my secretary while we waited on the leading of the Lord to the mission field. As we waited, we enjoyed everyday life in Toronto together. We joined FaithWay Baptist Church in Ajax, Ontario, developed many dear friendships, and were encouraged greatly by our pastor who faithfully presented the Word of God each week and friends who were loyal and separated unto the Lord.

One of our special friends was Tom, who also happened to be the auditor of our company. Tom was a highly educated man with the potential to make a lot of money by walking in the way of the world; yet, he put Christ first, willing to pay the price of obedience to God's Word—a price that included his wife divorcing him when she learned he had accepted Christ as Saviour. Tom and I established a once-a-month businessmen's luncheon, gathering Christian friends and inviting non-Christian businessmen to network in local hotels and restaurants where we were often able to share the gospel. When Tom later remarried a Christian lady named Cathy, Rosann and I developed a close friendship with the couple. We regularly prayed for each other, and Tom and I were partners in Thursday church visitation, braving harsh winter weather to knock on doors and warming up afterwards over a cup of hot coffee at McDonalds.

Despite the wonderful opportunities to serve Christ alongside dear people like Tom and Cathy and thoroughly enjoying our days in Canada, Rosann and I still felt we were "marking time" there, never able to get fully settled into our new life. Although we did not know when, all along we knew God would surely call us back to Lebanon. And one morning, our wait came to an end with a personal letter from a Lebanese friend. Reading the letter, I discovered that a young pastor in Lebanon whom I had known for many years had been sitting in his office studying the Bible and preparing a sermon with his son playing nearby, when a Muslim extremist burst into the church office with a pistol and began shooting. Although the assassin failed to kill Pastor Habib, a bullet hit his spinal cord and paralyzed him for life. Because of the limitations of care in Beirut's American University Hospital where he had been transported after the shooting, Pastor Habib had been flown to Rochester, New York, to receive better treatment.

The Lord used this letter to challenge my heart, gently reminding me that while I was enjoying a comfortable life and job in Canada, my friends in Lebanon were being persecuted in the service of the Lord. To me, this was God's clear call to go to Lebanon and fill the gap. I immediately called my wife at home and told her about the letter and my certainty that the Lord had just firmly called us to Lebanon. Rosann assured me that if the Lord had confirmed His call to me, we needed to take all the steps necessary to obey, and she was fully behind me in this decision.

Soon after, we announced to our church our calling to go back to Lebanon as missionaries. After the service, we stood at the back door as people came by to greet us and assure us of their prayers. Although excited with us for what God may do, many were amazed that we would be going to a war-torn country.

One lady—a dear widow and friend of ours, Mrs. Kennedy—reached into her purse and handed me a silver coin. I could tell it was a dear possession of hers which she had kept for many years.

As she pressed it into my hand, she told me she had been saving it for a special occasion or need. She wanted me to sell it and use the money, which she was confident would be a great amount, to get started as a missionary.

When I had the coin appraised, I learned that it actually did not have much value. But, to Rosann and me, it has great value—so much so that we decided it was too valuable to sell. We still have this coin, and every time we look at it, it reminds us of the poor widow, Mrs. Kennedy, and her love for the Lord and sacrifice that others might hear the gospel.

Of course, identifying God's leading and stepping out in obedience did not mean we could just drop everything and fly to Lebanon. Over the course of several months we resigned our jobs and sold our house. I completed the process to qualify and become ordained and commissioned at Southside Baptist Church in South Carolina, and Rosann and I joined World Wide New Testament Baptist Missions and began deputation to raise our support. In the middle of all this, on April 11, 1984, the Lord blessed us with a baby boy, whom we named Mitchell, after my father.

Rosann and I thoroughly enjoyed the deputation process, including driving to churches and sharing our burden with other believers. We actually found deputation exciting, with many opportunities to not only reap the benefit of support for the work in Lebanon, but also to see many people saved. I was able to speak in scores of churches, Christian schools, and high schools, and in spite of the bad economy in those days, we raised our support in the amazingly brief period of one and a half years, enabling us to head for Lebanon in the summer of 1985. The Lord provided us a home in Lebanon through a medical doctor—a surgeon—who offered to rent his house to us. He further answered our prayers about where to serve when the missionary who led me to Christ as a child contacted me and invited me to use the church he had built for our meetings, fearing that militias might occupy or destroy the building if it were left unattended. Thus, before we even left for Lebanon, the Lord had settled the issues of our ministry and home.

Now we needed to prepare ourselves mentally for the drastic change of moving overseas for life and ministry. The stability of the American life we had briefly known made it easy to take many things for granted, such as a constant supply of electricity, comfortably heated or cooled homes with private garages, wide and paved roads, and supermarkets with a great variety of well-stocked food at reasonable prices. I tried to prepare Rosann, telling her life outside the United States or Canada is completely different, and its norms are not maintained throughout most of the third world. In Lebanon, she would not find gasoline stations or convenience stores that were open at all hours, and she would soon learn what it meant to worry about electricity shortages and whether our home would be warm enough during the winter.

Once we had sold all the possessions we were not carrying with us and completed the final details of our move, we began saying our goodbyes. On moving day, some men from our church drove us to the airport with our luggage and the crates we were shipping ahead of us, and then we were off. Because the Beirut International Airport was permanently closed, we flew to Cyprus and from there took a boat into Beirut. We sailed overnight from Limosol to Port Juni, a small seaport located north of Beirut. The sea was rough, which made for an eventful journey. We were hopeful, however, that the war was about to end, and Lebanon would soon be at peace. Little did we realize we were sailing straight into harm's way and that the worst was yet to come. Nonetheless, we were at peace. We knew our lives were in the hands of the Lord and that He had plans for our future. Instead of worrying about what we could be heading into, we prayed for grace and strength to succeed and see many saved.

Early in the morning, as the boat reached the shores of Lebanon and the coastline began to appear in the distance, we climbed the deck to take pictures. From the deck, Lebanon seemed so very far away, but as we drew closer, we saw the mountains and below them the high-rise buildings. Rosann cried out, "Edgar, there are houses! I can see buildings!"

Confused, I asked what she had expected. With a sheepish grin, she replied that the American news coverage had convinced her all of Lebanon was a war-torn wasteland, and she had thought we would need to live in a tent, for lack of a permanent structure to call home. As amusing as the misunderstanding was, Rosann's answer further assured me of God's call in our family's life. Rosann was willing to serve the Lord in Lebanon even if we had to live in a tent. Inwardly, I marveled at Rosann's dedication, and I thanked God again for bringing us together.

Finally, the boat came to a rest in the seaport, and we disembarked and were welcomed excitedly by my brother and some local Christians who had been waiting for us. As we left the seaport, I marveled at the goodness of God who saw fit, after several years and many changes, to allow me to once again step onto the soil of my homeland. I could barely wait to see how He would work in and through us as we sought to serve Him effectively among these people who so desperately needed His salvation and restoring work in their lives.

Seven

GRACE UNDER FIRE

Within two weeks of arriving in Beirut, we were relatively settled into our new home and adjusting to life in Lebanon—finding our way to the supermarkets, learning how to get water, and generally becoming acquainted with our community. Given the instability of the times, we were thankful to the Lord that both the area we had moved into and the one in which we were eager to begin ministering were relatively safe.

I knew that any ministry that seeks to reach those in need must begin with the messenger seeking out people to tell about the Saviour, which meant I would spend much time simply knocking on doors. But I also knew Lebanon had been called the "graveyard of missions" because so many missionaries before us had struggled long and hard among these people, with just a few churches started or souls saved as a result. Now Lebanon was mired in the turmoil and fear brought on by a prolonged war, so I prayed that the Lord who had led us here would go before us and show us He was with us by softening the hearts of those who answered the doors so they would be open to hearing the Good News of the gospel.

One warm and sunny afternoon shortly after we arrived in Beirut, I drove through the thronging city traffic to a neighborhood where I would be knocking doors. I parked my car, picked up my Bible, and began going from door to door. Much to my joy, the people welcomed me into their homes. In every home, the husband, wife, and even the children sat down to listen politely as I shared the gospel. Several of the families asked if the war in Lebanon was mentioned in the Bible and whether or not we were living in the last days. This gave me opportunity to tell them about Jesus, the hope of nations, and remind them that life on Earth is temporary and we are pilgrims and strangers on this planet. The illustration I used was salvation as a passport to eternity. I told the people that mankind is on Earth to acquire a visa to the next life, but our passports must be stamped with the seal of the Holy Spirit in order to enter Heaven after leaving this temporary life. I told them that without this seal, we are destined to pay eternally for our sins in the terrible place called Hell, but that the Lord Jesus Christ shed His blood and died that we might never have to pay that price. I told them that God wants everyone to come to the knowledge of truth because Jesus is the way, the truth, and the life and no one can enter Heaven apart from Him.

That first day of visiting and knocking doors, I noticed one family in particular listened intently as I shared the gospel with them over a cup of Turkish coffee. I asked if they wanted to invite Christ into their hearts. When they nodded, I led them in a prayer of salvation and afterward invited them to come to church. I prayed again with the family before I departed, thanking God for specifically answering my prayer that morning in a most powerful way. He answered again and again as I visited several families that afternoon and more than one responded to the gospel, proving to me His desire to bless the ministry to which He had called us.

I continued going from door to door, so engrossed in witnessing to these families that I failed to realize the sun was setting and the day was rapidly coming to an end. As I finished presenting the gospel to one family, the husband asked where I lived. When I replied I lived in northern Beirut, he urged me to leave immediately to try to arrive home before it was too dark outside. He warned me that after dark, snipers from Muslim West Beirut began shooting and the area we were in would be exposed to their fire. I thanked him for the warning and made my way to my car, my heart overflowing with joy and thanksgiving to the Lord for the response of the people and the obvious thirst in their hearts to hear the Word of God. I could hardly wait to get home to share the good news with my wife.

Singing and praising the Lord, I started the engine and headed down narrow and empty streets, my headlights illuminating a bit of the evening darkness that had fallen on the city. Suddenly, I heard the crack of a gunshot, and a bullet flew over my car and into the walls of a building I was passing. Seconds later, another bullet whizzed past, this one much closer. By the time the third shot followed, I realized I was being targeted by a sniper.

I had no idea what I should do. If I sped up, that might alert more activity in my direction, but if I stopped the car in the empty street, surely that would make me an even easier target. I cried out to the Lord in fear, asking for protection and direction, and His still, small voice spoke to my heart: "Edgar, turn off the headlights." In my naiveté, I had failed to realize my headlights put me in the greatest danger no matter how quickly or slowly I drove. I immediately turned off the lights, and the next gunshots I heard were farther away. The sniper could no longer see me. My heart was so full of relief and thankfulness that it would not be contained inside the car. I rolled down the car window and shouted praise to the Lord for His deliverance. I continued driving in darkness for several blocks, then became alarmed again when I began to realize something large was lurching ahead in the distance, headed straight for me. Again I pleaded with my Heavenly Father for direction, and again He spoke simply to my heart: "Turn on the headlights."

How often we get into situations in which our minds stop functioning through ignorance or fear! When I turned on my lights, I instantly saw a group of army tanks heading toward me. They too had turned off their lights so as not to be detected. I immediately swerved to the side of the road and avoided a collision just in time, then sat on the roadside for a few moments as the gravity of the situation and these two escapes from death began to dawn on me. I thanked the Lord again for His mighty protection.

By the time I was out of the danger zone and safely home, it was late at night and my wife was waiting for me at the door, her face filled with anxiety. She told me I had been gone so long that she had begun to fear something had happened to me and had been praying for my safe return. I told her that I had almost been killed twice that night but had been spared by the mercy and grace of God. After a moment of stunned silence, Rosann threw her arms around me. We held each other and quietly prayed together, thanking the Lord for His protection.

Although I would not fully realize it for two years, one lesson I later learned because of the events of that night was that members of the body of Christ are connected in supernatural ways through the Holy Spirit of God. When one of the members is hurt or in danger, the Head of the body, who is our Saviour, alerts other members to unite in prayer. Two years later, my family had returned to America on furlough to visit a supporting church in New Jersey and report on our work in Lebanon. At the end of the service, as I stood by the pastor and shook hands with church members, a lady I had never met asked what I had been doing on a particular day two years before. I recalled my night of close calls in Beirut and told her on that date I had been facing grave danger. As we continued to talk, she told an incredible story. That very day, the Lord had clearly spoken to her heart with the word *Feghaly*, a name she had never heard before, and called upon her to pray. She knew this was not a common American word or name, and although a dictionary search and query of her husband and pastor turned up no clues as to what a "Feghaly" might be, the lady was nonetheless faithful to pray.

One month later, this lady visited a special service at another Baptist church in her area and out of curiosity shared her experience with the pastor of that church and asked if he were familiar with the word. The pastor immediately told her about my family and our missionary calling from the Lord to the war-torn country of Lebanon. He suggested the Lord may have laid our name on her heart because we were in some kind of danger or had a significant need. From then on, that dear lady was faithful to continue praying for me and my family, and two years later she could hardly contain her excitement as she told me her story. I listened to her in wonder, realizing that on one of the scariest nights of my life, on an empty street in Beirut and seemingly alone, the Lord had miraculously raised an army of prayer warriors to help protect me.

The Early Days

The encouragement I received from the Lord in the early days of the ministry through the softened hearts of those I visited and the faithfulness of other believers served to confirm my calling back to Lebanon. With the Lord going before me and my family by my side, I endeavored to continue serving the Lord and sharing His Word. Going door to door proved to be helpful in meeting those in our community and inviting many to our church. The church building in which we met had been constructed by the missionary who had led me to Christ while he was on the field, and, although it had noticeably deteriorated during the war, it was still sturdy enough to house our congregation, which then numbered about fifteen.

Our first church service in Beirut was on a Wednesday night, and it was certainly memorable. As was not uncommon, there was no electricity that night, so we used kerosene lamps to

light the building. The service opened with a prayer followed by
a few songs, after which I stood to preach. Right in the middle
of my sermon, our building shook with the force of explosions
as the neighborhood came under fire by the Syrian army and
hostile militias. Large mortar bombs exploded everywhere
around us, and almost on cue, everyone in the congregation
simply bent over and ducked their heads to avoid the shrapnel.

Looking back on that night, it seems funny that I was so
unsure of what to do. Amid the sudden chaos and noise of the
explosions, and although everyone else had ducked down and
out of harm's way, I went on preaching my sermon. I suppose
I was pretending to be unaffected by the commotion. A short
time later, someone called out for me to save the sermon for
later, come down from the pulpit, and join the congregation
on the floor. A little chagrined at my seeming bravado, I ran
to the pews to join my wife, who held her hands over the ears
of our fifteen-month-old son, Mitchell, in attempt to keep him
calm. Although we knew we were all in imminent danger and
a bomb could hit our building at any moment, we wanted to
shield him from the fear we felt. Seeing this, a lady in the pew
behind us—who, coincidentally, I had won to the Lord when
I was a teenager long before the war started and who was still
faithfully attending the church—reached out to Rosann and
said in broken English, "Don't afraid! Don't afraid!"

It seemed we waited amid the pews forever, listening and
praying as bombs continued to land around us. But we were
blessed to experience the protection of our Lord, and after a
time the bombing finally stopped. Shaken but determined, I
returned to the pulpit and finished the sermon.

Neither car bombs nor mortar bombs were going to deter us from attending and ministering in the church or from knocking on doors and witnessing to people who so desperately needed the hope of the Word of God. Beginning with our first Sunday service days later, I made it a practice to give a clear presentation of the gospel and an invitation for salvation each week. We rejoiced at seeing souls saved and our church beginning to grow as a result.

Gospel Fruit

Shortly after the bombing during our first midweek service, we had another church first: our first major revival meeting in 1986. In spite of, or perhaps because of, the war, people came every day to hear the Word of God. Every night the church was filled, and every night many raised their hands for salvation. The fruit of this revival opened my eyes to understand Jesus' parable of the sower in Matthew 13 as never before. In it, as the farmer carried the seed to sow, some fell by the roadside and the birds devoured it. Some seed fell on stony ground and because the soil had no depth, it withered away. Other seed fell among thorns and was choked by them. Some of the seed, however, fell upon good soil and flourished to produce fruit. As a missionary, I saw this parable lived out before my eyes in the lives of those who attended our little church. Many paid lip service or pretended to be Christians but fell away as time revealed their hearts. But others truly received the gospel, and their changed lives were testimony of the hope they gained in Christ.

One dear lady who came to Christ as a result of our ministry was a widow named Imm George. (*Imm* is a title that means "the mother of." Her firstborn son's name was George, so she was called Imm George. *Abou* as a title means "the father of." Sometimes I'm called Abou Mitchell.) Tragically, Imm George had already lost two of her sons in the war, but, if that were not enough, as her family hid in their home during yet another battle, her third son peered out of the window to see what was going on and was struck by shrapnel from a nearby exploding mortar bomb. His throat completely severed, he fell to the floor with his life blood gushing from him, his mother helpless to do anything but clutch her son and watch him die before her eyes. Imm George began to attend our church a short time after this devastating incident and was wonderfully saved. One day, I went to pay her a visit and comfort her with the Word of God. I read to her from Paul's second letter to the church in Corinth: "Therefore we are always confident, knowing that, whilst we are at home in the body, we are absent from the Lord: (For we walk by faith, not by sight:)We are confident, I say, and willing rather to be absent from the body, and to be present with the Lord" (2 Corinthians 5:6–8).

Imm George looked at me, face etched by pain, and told me the only thing preventing her from collapsing under the weight of her grief was the hope she found in Jesus Christ. She rejoiced that her Saviour had put a song in her heart in the midst of tragedy, and she found comfort and peace in the promises found in His Word.

What a thrill this lady's testimony brought to my heart. Her example was a valuable lesson to me that I did not need to remind people of the horror of Hell or the brevity of life. I did not even need to talk much about the afterlife because the people of Beirut knew full well that every day they remained alive was a mercy. Many became fatalists in an effort to maintain their sanity, and they just quit worrying about whether or not they would live. As missionaries during this dark time, we had the decided advantage of giving hopeless people wonderful news about a Saviour who came to bring hope. I challenged those around me that life on earth cannot be compared to eternity with the Lord in Heaven and that rejecting Jesus would condemn them to Hell, for once they died and entered eternity, the opportunity to be saved was lost forever. These simple facts made plain by the Word of God caused many to respond and receive Christ as Saviour.

One Sunday morning, a man named Kamil, who I later discovered was the leader of a militia group, attended our church. Kamil had a well-known reputation for being a cruel man who loved to hurt people, but somehow he found out about our church and sat quietly during the service. My sermon that Sunday was about Calvary and how the mighty God of the whole Earth chose to be born as a baby, then later went to Calvary and willingly shed His blood for our sakes so that we could benefit from His sacrifice by spending eternity in Heaven. During the invitation when I asked if any wanted to receive Him into their hearts, this man raised his hand.

Normally, a team of men and women would stand at the back of the church during the invitation to share the plan of salvation and pray with any who raised a hand. Afterward, the team members would take the new believer around to introduce them to others in the church. When Kamil raised his hand for salvation, however, none of the team wanted to pray with him. They were all too afraid of his bad reputation. When one of the deacons told me of the situation and asked me to step in and pray with this young man, I confess I initially doubted whether he was serious. I did my duty though, and he prayed with me and quietly followed me as I introduced him to several church members as a new believer.

The next day Kamil was leaving for work when he noticed his neighbor in his car, also preparing to leave for work, and the car's side view mirror on the ground. Kamil picked up the mirror and politely gave it to his neighbor, then continued down the street. The neighbor was so stunned by Kamil's good deed that he jumped out of his car and shouted after him, wanting to know why Kamil had treated him kindly instead of cruelly. Kamil shared that the day before, he had attended a Baptist church, heard about Christ, and had given his life to Jesus. From then on, Kamil continued, he would abandon all violence because he was a child of Christ.

The neighbor was so astounded that he asked to know more about the Saviour who could change even a man like Kamil. The next Sunday, Kamil's neighbor and his entire family attended our church, and all of them gladly received Christ. The blessed sequel to this story is that Kamil, this formerly cruel militia man, eventually surrendered his life to serve the Lord, and today pastors a church.

Another militia man I witnessed to had difficulty walking as a complication of being shot sometime earlier. His daughter, an active church member who loved the Lord, would regularly ask us to pray for her father. One day, I was led of the Lord to go witness to this man, and as we spoke, he expressed great anger against a God who would allow him to be shot and experience constant pain. I told him that as bad as his injury was, he could be thankful to God that the bullet had only damaged his body and not taken his life. He was still alive, which meant God had given him another chance to receive Christ as his Saviour. Instead of being comforted by my words, the man was enraged. A few days later, he sent a message that if I ever attempted to visit or come near him again, he would shoot and kill me.

What could I do but bring this man before the Heavenly Father in prayer? I asked every member of the church to pray daily that the Lord would open his eyes and show him his need of a Saviour. Not long afterward, a family problem developed between this man and his siblings that was so profound that it drove him to our church. When he entered the church building on a Sunday morning, I immediately recognized him and was thrilled, if also puzzled, to see him. I prayed this would be his day of salvation, and once again, God answered prayer. During the invitation, he raised his hand to be saved. I went through the plan of salvation with him personally and prayed with him. The salvation of this man, who had been known for his profanity and love of violence, sent a shock wave through the community. In an instant, his evil habits left him, replaced by praise, thanksgiving, and a desire to be a great witness for the Lord. As a result of his testimony, others in the area wanted to know more about the Saviour. Today, almost all of his children have accepted Christ, and one of them now pastors the church in Beirut.

Of course, not everyone was happy about the lives that God was changing in our community. Most notably, the Catholic Church showed its displeasure through intimidation tactics meant to silence new believers or sway them from their decisions to follow Christ. Lebanon is not like America, where there is greater freedom of religious choice. In Lebanon, the Orthodox and Catholic churches are very powerful. As the holders and executors of legal documents and binding relationships, they demand unquestioning loyalty of their members and exert tremendous pressure on any who choose to leave the Church.

One incident of intimidation involved a man in our church who was so excited upon receiving salvation that he simply could not keep his joy to himself. He began to tell all of the people in his village about the Saviour. Some of his neighbors were irritated by his zeal for Christ and reported him to the local Catholic priest, who literally threatened this man with physical persecution. In front of the man's entire household, the priest threatened to cut him into pieces if he continued witnessing about Christ. Undaunted, the man replied that every piece of his body, whether intact or not, would continue to praise and honor the Lord who had saved him. The priest switched tactics and told the man that continuing to witness for Christ would cost him a burial place in his family's cemetery, which was managed by the church. This new brother in Christ responded that it did not matter where his body was buried because his soul would be with Jesus.

Several other church members reported similar threats. On one occasion, a widow and her daughter who had been faithfully attending our church were suddenly absent for a couple of weeks, prompting Rosann and me to visit them out of concern. During our visit, we learned the local priest had threatened them and demanded they attend mass at the Greek Orthodox Church. Considering the great power of the Church, these ladies did not know how to respond. I told them that I understood their struggle and would not argue if they bent to the pressure to return to the Orthodox Church. I reminded them that once believers trust Christ, He lives in their hearts forever, regardless of what church they attended. However, I urged them to make sure whatever they chose was pleasing to the Lord.

The next Sunday, I was delighted to see the widow and her daughter in church, looking happy and singing with obvious joy. After the service, I asked how they had made their decision to come back to church. The widow explained she had asked an unsaved relative for advice about the situation, and after confirming she was a true believer in Christ, the widow had been surprised to hear the unsaved relative quote Scripture, telling her that Jesus Himself had said, "If any man will come after me, let him deny himself, take up his cross daily, and follow me" (Luke 9:23). At this wise advice from an unexpected source, the widow had concluded the Lord wanted her to be in the church where they had been saved and where they would be spiritually fed.

The converts we saw in Lebanon thrilled our hearts as they left their old lives and dedicated themselves to the cause of Christ. Many suffered persecution at the hands of their own relatives or former churches, but their steady faithfulness to the Lord was and still is a testament to the working of the Holy Spirit and the power of Christ through salvation.

Eight

SMILING IN THE STORM

One of the most valuable lessons I've learned in my life is that every Christian must carry the yoke Christ gives to each of us. If we carry our God-given yokes and minister according to the Lord's will and calling rather than our own preferences, no matter how heavy the yoke or how difficult the ministry, we will find His yoke is easy and brings incredible joy.

I am ever grateful to the Lord who called me to minister and enabled me to serve Him in Lebanon. He truly provided spiritually, emotionally, and physically for my family's every need. The home we acquired in Lebanon that belonged to the surgeon in New York proved to be a great blessing. It was located near the American Embassy in an area not directly targeted by Muslim militias, and many Embassy employees lived close by. Some were Christians, and when they discovered we drank American coffee, they started coming to our home to have a cup or brought us bags of coffee from the States. Rosann and I were greatly encouraged by their faith and fellowship, and we were deeply saddened when it became necessary that they be evacuated from Lebanon.

A Growing Ministry

Because the area of our church was so often bombed or otherwise attacked at night, like most of the other churches, we did not hold evening services. Instead, Rosann and I opened our home on Sunday afternoons to receive believers and friends. We even bought a ping-pong table for our little backyard so the young people could play while the adults fellowshipped over refreshments or gathered to sing around the piano. These times were an oasis in the midst of the hard day-to-day life in Lebanon.

Our Sunday afternoon fellowships proved fruitful as many strangers and unbelievers also found their way to our house. As we gradually established friendships and gained their trust, they began to ask spiritual questions that gave us opportunities to witness to them about the Saviour. During this period of our ministry, Rosann baked more cake and brewed more coffee than at any other time in our lives, but it was such a special time. We would not have had it any other way.

Our house was on the northern side of Beirut while the church was on the southern side, which gave us opportunity to pass through many areas on our way to church. As we drove through the streets of Beirut, Rosann and I often noticed many Africans walking the streets. Later, we discovered they had come to work in Lebanon, often working jobs the Lebanese natives refused to do, such as factory work for the men or work in local homes as servants for the women. They lived in their own community and had no personal interaction with the Lebanese. Often, a group would rent a house, with two or three people sharing each room. In many cases, women would share a room with a man to whom they were not married. Many of them were alcoholics, finding sad comfort in drink. The Lord began to lay a burden on our hearts for these dear people, but we did not know how to approach them and win their trust, considering they generally did not associate with Lebanese.

One day when I pulled into our local gas station, a young African man came to fill up my tank. When he finished and I had paid for the gas, I asked if he spoke Arabic and learned that he spoke English. I gave him an English tract entitled "God's Plan for Salvation." He received it politely, examined it, and then asked me what I did. I told him I was a Baptist minister and pastored a church in Southern Beirut. He surprised me by asking if he could come visit me at my home after work, and I of course told him he was welcome. That afternoon when he visited us at home, I learned he was a Muslim from Ghana in West Africa and his name was Mohammed Ali Abina. Someone had told him about the Lord while he was in Ghana, and, as is so often the case when God prepares a heart, I experienced a real freedom when I witnessed to him. We spoke of Mohammed, the founder of Islam, versus the Lord Jesus; the Islamic Holy Book, the Koran, versus the Bible; and salvation by works versus salvation by grace. When I finished showing him the differences and presenting the gospel, I was able to lead him in prayer for salvation.

Mohammed Ali Abina's first decision after receiving Christ as Saviour was to change his name to Joe. I soon noticed that Joe possessed genuine leadership qualities and was a man of great integrity. I felt in my heart that he might be the God-appointed answer to my prayer about connecting with Lebanon's African community. I bombarded Joe with questions about Africans in Lebanon and the nature of their work, and I learned that most worked throughout the week and finished on Saturday at noon. At that, I invited Joe to come to our home every Saturday afternoon for a Bible study and prayer meeting and hastened to add that he could bring any African friends with him.

Joe was excited to come, and the following Saturday he brought a friend with him. As word spread about our Bible study, more Africans began to attend. One man was named Foster, and he belonged to an Islamic sect called Ahmadia. Foster had been attending Jehovah's Witness meetings since he had come to Lebanon, and when he visited our church he asked me if I could show him from the Bible that Jesus is God. After I proved this fact to him from Scripture, Foster gladly received salvation, left the Jehovah's Witnesses to begin faithfully attending our Saturday afternoon Bible study, and later surrendered his life to serve the Lord.

Another man, named Peter, had tried to go to a few Lebanese churches in the area before attending our Bible study but had found that neither the people nor the ministers of those churches would even shake his hand. Frustrated at this treatment, he was about to give up on Christianity, when he heard about our church in Haddath, Beirut. The very first time he visited, everyone welcomed him and made him feel at home.

His testimony later revealed that it was the love he saw in our church that inspired him to continue to come. Later, by the grace of God, Peter also surrendered his life in service to God.

As more people started coming to our Bible study, it became obvious that our home would not hold everyone, so we began to look for a larger house to rent. In time, we found a suitable one with enough bedrooms for Africans to sleep and a living room large enough to be used for a church.

The Lord blessed our ministry to the African people in a mighty way, and we began to see an average of a hundred Africans attending church on Sundays. I began using a bus that we had received from a church in the States to bring many of them to church. The bus seated twenty-four passengers, but we filled it over capacity every week to carry about seventy Africans to church, and those trips were so boisterous with joyful hymn singing and praising God that it was a wonder we were never stopped by the militias. These African believers grew wonderfully in the Lord, and they were a constant source of joy, not only to Rosann and me, but also to the Lebanese believers who attended.

Many times in those days I would think back to the moment in 1978 when I sat in the snack shop at Bob Jones University with the young lady who would later become my wife and asked her what she wanted to do with her life. She had considered carefully before answering that, although she was not sure, she thought she might like to be a missionary to Africa. I had asked her if she might be interested in ministering in Lebanon, which was not far from Africa, and she had smiled at me.

"Well, that should do," she told me.

My wife was faithful to serve with me in Lebanon, and just a few years after that day in the snack shop, God gave Rosann the desire of her heart and brought Africa to her. How true the words of the psalmist, found in my wife's life verse: "Delight thyself also in the Lord: and he shall give thee the desires of thine heart" (Psalm 37:4).

An Unexpected Surprise

The growth and development of the African ministry was a source of much joy to us in those days, but another major event that occurred at the same time also brought us cause for great rejoicing. In late 1985 my wife and I discovered we were expecting our second child, our precious daughter, Julie. This news brought great joy to our family.

Amid the excitement of expecting our daughter, things in Lebanon were more tense than ever. The civil war seemed to be taking a different direction, as more sophisticated and deadly weapons flowed through the country and into the hands of both Muslim and Christian militias. In truth, the conflict could no longer be described as a civil war; by 1986, it was an international war. Countless Muslim Arab extremists flocked into Lebanon with financing and weapons of their own to join the "holy war" against the Christians. Christian and other groups received backing from other world powers to repulse their attacks.

In the streets of Lebanon, conflict was generally sporadic with periods of calm interrupted when snipers would begin firing indiscriminately at people. A sure indication that we needed to brace for a battle was when the sniper fire was followed by scattered car bombs and mortar bombs exploding. Next would come a total blackout across the city, the cutoff of the water supply, and then the closing of gasoline stations and supermarkets. Because supplies of fuel and food were completely dependent on the length of the battle, merchants remained open only as long as they had products to sell. Thus, as soon as we heard the report of sniper fire, we hurried to the store to stock up, then filled plastic five-gallon containers with gasoline, which we stored in the coolest portion of our homes: the bathroom, where there were no windows. We filled our bathtubs with water for bathing and other purposes, then traveled up to the mountains to fill as many jugs as we could with fresh drinking water from the springs. Dirty dishwater was saved in buckets to be used later for flushing toilets, and we made sure to wash all of our clothes in anticipation of going long periods without water.

The Christian area was heavily attacked by Muslim militias in early April 1986, provoking a heavy response from Christian militias anxious to demonstrate their might. This proved to be one of the most vicious battles of the war, with both militias incorporating every weapon they had available to them. Cannon and mortar bombs, rocket-propelled grenades, and missiles rained from the skies, spreading devastation and death everywhere.

Rosann was nine months along and due any day. We had no idea exactly when her labor might begin, so we prayed the baby would wait until the battle subsided. Several people from our church had taken refuge in our home, and they were also praying desperately Julie would not be born that day. But as

April 26, 1986, dawned with a violent exchange of fire, Rosann quietly told me our daughter would wait no longer. As the morning progressed, I feared it would be impossible to drive her to the hospital. We knew of no doctor near us who could make a house call, and the hospitals were full of people injured in the battle. But when the time comes, battle or no battle, a baby must be born, so we once again asked the Lord to intervene as we had done so often in desperate times before.

As we waited into the afternoon, Rosann's contractions began in earnest. The rest of us were glued to the radio listening for political and military developments. Early that evening, when the tension of waiting and fearing was so thick it was almost visible, a newsflash came across the airwaves, interrupting the regular programming. There had been a complete cessation of hostilities between the militias on both sides of the city, and all militias would hold their fire. Those of us huddled around the battery radio shouted jubilantly, for our prayers had been answered. Our Heavenly Father had commanded a halt to the violence so our little girl could be born safely.

We contacted our doctor, who asked us to meet him immediately at the hospital. Without the constant pounding of bombs and rifle fire, the roads were strangely quiet as we traveled, but we saw their damage everywhere, and could only thank and praise the Lord that the roads were safe enough for us to be out in the open. About an hour later we arrived at the hospital to find our doctor and a medical team waiting to take Rosann directly to the delivery room. Later that evening, we met our beautiful, healthy baby girl for the first time, born in a God-given moment of peace amid the chaos of war.

The Storm Worsens

Since my salvation, I have done my best to read my Bible every day. I believe the more that Christians read the Word of God, the more we come to understand His mind and His will for our lives. In the process of reading, whenever God speaks to me through a particular verse, I endeavor to memorize it. In this manner, I memorized and have come to treasure Psalm 91. When I was young, I could not fully comprehend the meaning and power of the promises this chapter contains about the might and wisdom of God and His care for His children. But Psalm 91 came alive and proved true for me during the Lebanese War, and two verses in particular, "He shall cover thee with his feathers, and under his wings shalt thou trust: his truth shall be thy shield and buckler. Thou shalt not be afraid for the terror by night; nor for the arrow that flieth by day" (Psalm 91:4–5).

When I was a child, I thought these verses were merely symbolic, but my experiences during the war showed me God meant every word. He provided His divine protection and safety during the terror of bombs falling by night and the arrow of sniper shots that killed dozens of innocent people around us by day. I learned that Psalm 91 is a comforting reality, providing peace and security in the most frightening circumstances. Thus, I considered serving the Lord in Lebanon a holy privilege and calling, and I trusted without doubt that He would hold my family safely in the palm of His hand.

The fierce battle of 1986 only added to the damage our neighborhood had sustained in previous conflicts, which led to an interesting conversation with our building manager. He came to see me because, of the many bombs that had landed around the building we lived in, none had hit the building itself. This man was a staunch Catholic and worshipper of Catholic saints, and he knew I was a Baptist minister who believed only the Bible. I had witnessed to him many times in the past, explaining to him that worship belongs to the Lord alone and that Jesus Himself had told Satan, "Thou shalt worship the Lord thy God, and him only shalt thou serve" (Matthew 4:10b).

I was not too surprised when the building manager came to visit that day and began conversation by pointing to the statue of Mary adorning our building and announcing that Saint Mary had protected us from the bombs that devastated other areas of our neighborhood. I told him I understood his love for Mary, but in order for her to protect us, she would have to be omniscient, omnipresent, and omnipotent—characteristics only God possesses. I asked if he believed Mary was God, and he shook his head. Then I opened my Bible and showed him that God's Word plainly demonstrates that Jesus is God the Son who came to Earth and died for us. I went on to show him what the Bible says about eternal life and Heaven, explaining that it is the Lord who protects His children because He is the living, eternal God.

I told him that if Mary were alive today, she would tell all those who persist in worshipping her that the only one truly deserving of worship and honor is the Lord Jesus, who told His disciples, "I am the way, the truth, and the life: no man cometh unto the Father, but by me" (John 14:6). The man did not accept Christ that day, but the seed of the Word of God was truly planted in his heart.

During that tumultuous year, the Lord provided His miraculous protection many times over. On one occasion, Rosann and I were returning home from visitation. We passed a supermarket we frequented, and my wife reminded me we were short on coffee and should stop and buy some in case guests came to visit. Our home was always open to people, and guests would think nothing of showing up unannounced, even late into the evening, for a visit over coffee. This particular supermarket was one of the few local retailers that sold Folgers, the American coffee I preferred and would normally never turn down a chance to buy. But for some reason, that day I was hesitant. I told her we would come back another day for the coffee, and we continued driving toward home.

Half a mile down the road, as we reached the top of a bridge, our car was suddenly and violently shaken, and our ears pounded with intense pressure. In the rearview mirror I saw a familiar sight: a huge pillar of fire erupting with smoke and debris. Like any other Lebanese resident, I knew the law of survival dictated we leave that area as quickly as possible, so I floored the accelerator. The moment we arrived home, we hurried inside and turned on the radio to learn that a female terrorist had been driving a car filled with explosives on a timer, intending to target the nearby army barracks. However, because of the heavy traffic, she grew frightened that the bomb would detonate prematurely, so she parked the car in the supermarket lot, then abandoned it and fled. The explosion had completely destroyed the supermarket—and had we been inside, we would have been numbered among the casualties.

As we considered how close to death we had come but for the goodness and protection of God, we felt mixed emotions. While we were thankful for the opportunity to serve the Lord in Lebanon, this incident had just further confirmed we could die at any moment. We felt an ever-increasing need to exercise wisdom with this fact in mind. We telephoned two ministers we knew in America who had good homes and asked them to adopt our children in the event we were killed in the Lebanese War. We did not want our children to remain in Lebanon should something happen to us. Of course, both pastors readily agreed, promising to care for our children as their own. Those assurances greatly comforted us even though we continued to experience the Lord's protection and were never harmed during all the dangerous days of the conflict.

Throughout the late 80s and early 90s, the violence in Lebanon continued to escalate, especially whenever the Christian (Catholic) Lebanese Army and Lebanese Forces, both of whom were supposed to be protecting East Beirut, began fighting each other. As a result, a new line of demarcation had been created, making the drive from our home to church much more dangerous, as we lived in a village controlled by the Christian Lebanese Army and separated from the Lebanese Forces by a valley. By that time, the Christian side of Lebanon had become so experienced in war tactics that it was well able to defend itself against any opponent, including the Syrian Army, but it was steadily weakened by the division between the Army and the Forces.

Early one cold February morning, a Lebanese soldier knocked on our door and politely asked us to crack open our windows. He explained his tank was parking just outside our building, and if it should have to fire its cannon, the concussion might shatter our windows. When the rest of our building learned about the tank, everyone wanted to go down to examine it and talk with the soldiers. The soldiers were friendly to us. They pointed to the hill across from our house and told us they were awaiting orders to fire at the militias on the other side of the hill.

Our son, Mitchell, always an eager, excitable child, jumped up and down, waving his hands with excitement. The officer noticed him and asked if he would like to climb up on the tank. Seeing my son's joy and without thinking it through, I gave him permission. The officer pulled him up and sat him behind the anti-aircraft machine gun. Mitchell began to pull the machine gun to the left and right, pretending he was one of the soldiers and fighting an enemy. The officer warned him not to touch the gun's trigger or else the gun would discharge, sending bullets to the opposite hill and starting the battle.

Doubtless, Mitchell did not fully realize the implication of the officer's words, but they jolted me. I realized that while our neighbors and my son stood happily admiring the tank and the soldiers, we were in real danger. One slip, and the militias on the other side would immediately respond. Furthermore, every apartment in our building was filled with gallons of gasoline stored as stockpiles to fuel our cars because the gas stations had been closed. Should even one projectile hit an apartment in the building, the entire place would be turned into a massive firebomb.

I quietly called Rosann up to our bedroom where we knelt and prayed for the Lord's protection, asking Him yet again for a miracle. We knew the soldier outside was awaiting an order to shoot, and we prayed earnestly that God would intervene so that order would never come. All through the day we expected the tank to shoot its cannon, but nothing happened. As night fell, our children were playing on our balcony when we heard them shouting, "Goodbye, tank! Goodbye, tank!" We hurried to the door to see the tank quietly leaving with its headlights extinguished.

Two days later, the tank officer returned to the village. He explained to us that every time the tank was sent on a mission, soldiers always used its ammunition in order to return to the base at a lighter weight. He remarked that this was the first time he had been sent on a mission and had not used any ammunition. Rosann and I thanked God for intervening for us, and I remembered His promise in Psalm 91:14–15, "Because he hath set his love upon me, therefore will I deliver him: I will set him on high, because he hath known my name. He shall call upon me, and I will answer him: I will be with him in trouble; I will deliver him, and honour him."

By May of 1990, hostilities in the Middle East were still mounting as Iraq celebrated victory over Iran and prepared to fight against Kuwait. Meanwhile, tensions in Lebanon were also growing as the Christian Army and the Lebanese Forces seemed to be gearing up for a final confrontation. We stored up water and gasoline to prepare for shortages and kept updated on news about the war as we could, but it was obvious that Lebanon was becoming increasingly dangerous.

One morning in May, we sent our children to school as usual, and then Rosann and I visited some local families then ran a few errands. As we drove toward the southern part of the city, we noticed there was an unusual amount of army movement and blockades set up everywhere. As we conducted our errands, we noticed people in the shops around us looking nervous. The lines at the bakery and supermarket were much longer than normal. We immediately went on full alert—something was about to happen.

We postponed the rest of our errands and headed back to the school to pick up the children. As we drove, we began to hear explosions, which added to our haste, and by the time we reached the school, bombs were landing nearby. Inside, we found children and teachers hiding under the stairwell, and Mitchell and Julie were huddled together, holding hands. The moment our children spotted us, they anxiously darted toward us, and we told the teachers we were taking them home. As we ran to our car, Mitchell began to cry because he had left his books in his classroom. Rosann urged me to forget the books, but I realized if the school were bombed, the cost to replace those books would be very high. I took my son by the hand, and we calmly reentered the building to retrieve his books, then returned to the car.

Yet another battle had begun by the time we arrived home, and this one raged for two days—during which the teachers and children at the school who had not left at the same time we did were trapped inside the school, unable to venture outside for fear of being caught in the violence. Once again, the Lord's wise prompting had delivered us, and we praised

Him for His goodness, agreeing with the psalmist, "Surely he shall deliver thee from the snare of the fowler, and from the noisome pestilence. Because thou hast made the Lord, which is my refuge, even the most High, thy habitation; There shall no evil befall thee, neither shall any plague come nigh thy dwelling" (Psalm 91:3, 9–10).

We relied more than ever on God's protection as it soon became apparent that even staying off the streets and in our homes would not bring much safety from the fighting. We frequently heard of terrorists knocking on doors of homes and gunning down anyone who answered, so we quickly learned to look through the peephole before opening our doors. But Mitchell and Julie, our friendly children who loved having visitors to our home and would race each other to the door to be the first to welcome our guests, were much too small to reach the peephole. For their safety, we installed a lock on the top of the door so they could not open it, giving an adult enough time to arrive and screen visitors.

We were also concerned to hear that terrorists were resorting to kidnapping individuals and making exorbitant ransom demands. Children who were not vigilantly supervised made easy targets, and while a church should have been a safe haven for children to socialize and play together, as ours loved to do with their friends, we were keenly aware that our church was situated just two short blocks from the line of demarcation and the stronghold of Hezbollah and the Shiite Muslims. Rosann and I wanted Mitchell and Julie to be able to have fun with their friends and not be afraid of what was going on around them, but we began to keep a constant watch over their activities. I specifically asked Rosann to never let them out of her sight while we were at church.

Through the danger, we continued our ministries, visitation, and soulwinning, feeling they were more needed than ever. I was intensely aware that more and more people were dying and entering eternity having never heard about the Saviour. This was not for a lack of religious presence in the area—the Catholic and Greek Orthodox churches believed in the trinity, the deity of Christ, and the Bible (though they hardly read it). But their churches never preached the gospel of Jesus Christ as Saviour, and their religion was drowning in traditions and church ceremonies. I needed a strategy to effectively bring the gospel to the 250,000 people of Haddath, most of whom claimed to be Christians but were clueless about the truth.

After much prayer and thought, I decided on a three-step outreach strategy. First, I would mobilize our church members with tracts and New Testaments, divide them into teams, and send each team to a different part of the city to knock on doors and talk to people about the gospel. At the beginning, some church members feared the people would think they were Jehovah's Witnesses and react badly, but to their surprise, when people found out they were not Jehovah's Witnesses, they welcomed church members into their homes and were open to hearing the Bible read to them. Thus, every home in our area was left with a tract or a New Testament and an invitation to visit our church.

The second step in the strategy was to have our church engage in personal follow-up witnessing and outreach to those who had invited us into their homes. Many of our church members came on Tuesdays and Thursdays to go out witnessing and to answer questions about the Bible and the Lord. We also hosted summer camps for many unsaved people, with teaching from the Word of God during the day and preaching about salvation during the evening. These camps proved very fruitful because people were glad to leave the chaos of war and retreat somewhere relatively safe to hear the Bible.

The third step in my plan to evangelize Haddath was to institute home Bible studies like our home study that had become so well-attended. Because of the violence in the streets, many people were afraid to go to church, so I believed we should take church to the people and make it easier for them to hear the Word of God. I began with one house meeting, then other men of our church learned how to lead these meetings and took charge of starting other home groups. At one time, we were holding eleven house meetings every week throughout our community, adding by extension an additional forty-five to our congregation who would not have otherwise attended.

As before, while we rejoiced in God's blessing and the growth of our ministry, not everyone in our community felt the same. Often, some who did not like what we were doing for the Lord would throw stones at the windows of the church or members' cars. Once, as I stood with my son beside me in the parking lot, a rock flew across the front of the church, landing on a car parked a few feet from us. When one of the deacons shouted that our church was being stoned, my reaction was to praise the Lord. At his confusion, I explained that in the thirty years our building had been standing, no one had thrown even so much as a flower, but that day they threw stones because we were winning souls and knocking on doors to tell people about the Saviour. Obviously, the devil was intimidated by what we were doing for Christ. But throwing stones was not going to stop us from bringing the Good News to people in darkness.

Our lack of response or retaliation, combined with our consistency in witnessing and serving the Lord, led to an eventual decrease in the number of attacks against us. Later, we were encouraged when some of the attackers even started attending our church. I discovered that the Lord can bring joy to our hearts even during the darkest storms. The Bible never promises that believers will be free from problems, difficulties, or tribulations; in fact, Jesus essentially guaranteed that we will have them: "These things I have spoken unto you, that in me ye might have peace. In the world ye shall have tribulation: but be of good cheer; I have overcome the world" (John 16:33). Yet, no matter what we go through, God promised never to leave us nor forsake us (Hebrews 13:5).

As a child, I learned a song that has often encouraged my heart during tumultuous times:

> *Begone, unbelief;*
> *my Saviour is near,*
> *and for my relief*
> *will surely appear;*
> *by prayer let me wrestle,*
> *and he will perform;*
> *with Christ in the vessel,*
> *I smile at the storm.*

With the promise of Christ's presence, we cannot only weather any storm—we can smile through it.

Nine

SPIRITUAL WARFARE

When I was growing up, I remember reading in the Bible the account of the man of Gadara whom Jesus delivered from demon possession (Mark 5:1–20). While I knew that all the Bible was true, it was hard to imagine such a situation in real life. In our home, we never spoke about demon possession, nor did I ever meet anyone possessed by demons. The closest I came was the occasional meeting of a supposed fortune teller or palm reader far outside our circle of acquaintances. When I began serving in Lebanon as a missionary, the Lord opened my eyes to the reality of the phenomenon of demon possession in our community. In fact, I discovered it was quite common, especially in the Muslim society, and it would not be long before I would see it with my own eyes.

On one occasion, our church had just concluded a Wednesday evening service and the congregation was dispersing, when two jeeps suddenly pulled up and stopped in front of our church building. Nearly two dozen armed men emerged and proceeded to rush inside. I was nearly frozen with shock, fearing they planned to harm us, until I saw one of our church members accompanying them. The member asked me to tell these men about Jesus and His salvation, and I was happy to do so—after the men agreed to lay aside their weapons, as this was the Lord's house and place of worship. To my amazement, they promptly placed their weapons in the rear of the church before settling themselves on the front pews. I delivered a simple gospel message, and when I invited them to receive Christ, I was stunned to see all of the men raise their hands for salvation. I wondered what on earth could have prompted them to seek out the Word of God and respond so emphatically.

The church member who accompanied them explained they had recently been shaken by their latest encounter with a man who regularly visited their militia base. This man appeared to have supernatural powers that could only have been given him by demons, and the soldiers became deeply frightened when he demonstrated his power by picking a fight with one of their men and then setting him on fire. This man continually and confidently confronted the troops, and each time his powers rendered the otherwise capable soldiers, helpless around him. But the men noticed his evil powers seemed to be hampered when our church member happened to show up to visit to a friend on the base. Our church member explained this was because the demon-possessed man had obviously sensed the authority of the Almighty God and then he told them about the

Saviour, of whom the Bible says, "greater is he that is in you than he that is in the world" (1 John 4:4b).

The leader of the militia in that base, being heartily tired of the demon-possessed man, expressed a desire to come meet me and learn more. When he visited our church and saw how we believed and used the Bible, he asked me if we could set this demon-possessed man free so he would stop persecuting them. I answered that we would pray over this man in the name of the Lord Jesus because He, and not I, had the power to cast out demons. We arranged for the militia leader to bring the demon-possessed man to our church, realizing that the success or failure of this meeting would affect the lives of all the militia, I asked two men in our church to join me in prayer and fasting before he arrived. My prayer was the Lord would show these troops His power and might through the prayers of His people.

Not long afterward, the militia leader and three of his men returned to the church, bringing the demon-possessed man with them. The man who was the cause of their trouble was quite young, and when he saw me and the others, he looked very afraid. I learned that he had gotten his power from his father, who had also been involved in the occult, and I couldn't help but suspect he had never been happy to possess it. I asked if he wanted to be set free of the evil hold on his life, and he responded positively. We began to pray in the name of the Lord Jesus, claiming the blood of Christ. As we prayed, the young man began to behave bizarrely. He suddenly spun around and laid hands on me and my prayer partners, attempting unsuccessfully to set us on fire. Clearly, the demons inside him had been disturbed. Next, he grabbed the open Bible in my hand and tried to set it on fire, and again, he was powerless to do so. The militia men who had watched their comrades suffer by this same tactic watched in amazement that he was unable to do anything to us.

As we continued to pray, the demon-possessed man seemed to be enduring intense internal struggle, to the point of almost losing consciousness. Suddenly, smoke rose from his hair, and before our astonished eyes, flames began to lick upward from his head. Unable to use him against us, the evil spirit controlling this young man had turned on him and set him on fire. We stopped praying, afraid that if we continued, Satan would kill or seriously harm him. We allowed him to leave but asked him to come again the following day. The militia leader was still open-mouthed in amazement at seeing firsthand the power of Christ at work. He freely admitted he had never seen anything like that before.

Sadly, the demon-possessed man never returned to the church. On his way home, the devil threatened to kill both him and his father if he came again to meet us. Although we had told him Satan is a liar and the father of lies (John 8:44) and that God could set him free, the young man chose to believe his lies and thus continued in slavery. Nonetheless, we still rejoiced that the Lord had used this occasion to demonstrate His protecting hand so the militia men could witness the power of God.

Another experience involved the family of a young lady living near our church who had grown up as a Maronite Catholic. Her father, who was involved in a shady business and was always careful to carry his pistol everywhere he went for physical safety, believed along with many others in Lebanon that communicating with spirits and demons was an attractive pastime. He learned too late that Satan always betrays his followers and abandons them to failure and destruction.

As this man grew older, he became sick and bed-ridden. One day, his wife heard him shouting and cursing as if he were engaged in an upsetting conversation with someone, and when she went to check on him, she was surprised to find him arguing with someone she could not see. When she asked her husband what was going on, he told her ugly creatures were trying to steal his food and were laughing at him when he demanded they leave him alone. Believing he was hallucinating from his illness, she assured him there was no one else in the room, but the man's tormentors were very real and kept coming to his room. I could not help but think that because this man had spent his life dabbling in the occult, perhaps these creatures knew his life was ending and they took pleasure in taunting him to Hell.

When days passed and the man's continued arguing with and cursing at creatures only he could see reached the point of preventing his family from sleeping at night, his wife went to their priest for help. He readily agreed to help and arranged to visit the home. Relying on the traditions of the Catholic Church, the priest recited the "Our Father" and "Hail Mary" prayers several times while walking around the man's bed, sprinkling it and the room with holy water. He waved his censer all around the room and the rest of the house, anointed the man with holy oil, and then left, assuring the wife that things would improve. When nothing changed and the poor man continued being tormented by the creatures, his wife and family members returned to the priest and asked if he could do something more.

The priest answered that the Church had exhausted its resources and there was nothing more he could do.

One day, the man began screaming for help, telling his family the creatures were coming to take him and he did not want to go with them. The apparent presence of these demons and the man's screaming were so horrifying that everyone in the household ran away from the home. When they returned a few hours later to check on him, the house was quiet, and the door to the man's room was locked. The door lock had long ago been broken and was thus never used. Confused and afraid, they broke down the door to discover the man inside cold and dead.

This man's daughter was so terrified that she began having nightmares every night. They continued even after she married, until one day she accepted an invitation to come to our church, where she heard the gospel for the first time and gladly responded to it along with her husband. The moment she surrendered to Christ, her nightmares stopped, never to be repeated. According to this lady's testimony, Jesus came into her heart, and the power of darkness moved out of her life. As she and her husband grew in grace, they became active members of our church, and her husband became a deacon and an effective witness for Christ.

A Cultic Opposition

Another demonic force we confronted in Lebanon was through those who had been influenced by cults. The Apostle John wrote in his first epistle, "Beloved, believe not every spirit, but try the spirits whether they are of God: because many false prophets are gone out into the world. Hereby know ye the Spirit of God: Every spirit that confesseth that Jesus Christ is come in the flesh is of God: And every spirit that confesseth not that Jesus Christ is come in the flesh is not of God: and this is that spirit of antichrist, whereof ye have heard that it should come; and even now already is it in the world" (1 John 4:1–3).

Just as Christians are influenced by the Holy Spirit as we read God's Word, there are evil spirits who motivate false prophets to misinterpret the Bible and to teach their false doctrines. During the first century of church history, the subtle Gnostics' doctrine produced a perversion of the true doctrine by denying the incarnation of the Lord Jesus Christ. This is what prompted John to warn believers about the importance of recognizing true prophets from false and the spirit of Christ from the spirit of anti-Christ. Although 1 John 4 was written hundreds of years ago, the central issue John warned about is the same today. An anti-Christ spirit will continue to control false teachers and deceive the vast majority of people about who Jesus Christ is until the Antichrist appears on Earth.

False teachings and deceptions about Christ include denying His virgin birth and deity, His death and resurrection, and His redemption of sins. These deceptions abound today in false religions like Islam, which acknowledges Jesus as a prophet and teacher but denies His deity, death, and resurrection. Muslims see Him as a prophet equal to Moses, Adam, and Muhammad, as do the Mormons, Jehovah's Witnesses, Scientologists, and every other theological cult in human history.

In 1 Timothy 4:1, the Apostle Paul further explains cultic behavior: "Now the Spirit speaketh expressly, that in the latter times some shall depart from the faith, giving heed to seducing spirits, and doctrines of devils;" Paul is saying that false doctrines appeal to the old sinful nature of man, not to the new nature that is born of the Spirit of God. These "seducing spirits" are demons that give people false hope, and because Satan is an imitator and his doctrines imitate those of Christ, many people believe they are worshipping the God of Heaven but instead are worshipping false gods. This is why so many religious people seem content with their ceremonies and traditions and have no interest in surrendering to Christ in faith and trusting in Him.

Our ministry in Lebanon was constantly filled with numerous encounters and conflicts with different cults and people who had been deceived by them. I discovered early on that Christians must be always on guard and prepared to testify of the hope and deliverance only found in Christ. I further discovered that the more battles we fight for Christ, the stronger we become in His strength and the weaker the enemy will become.

Once a man came to my home, accompanied by a friend of mine, and announced he had come to evangelize me. He told me he had joined a group (obviously a cult) that originated in Germany and taught that people can do whatever they please in life, including living in sin and immorality, and if they died and went to Hell, God would give them opportunity to repent and go to Heaven. This man was completely convinced what he was saying was true. He expressed genuine sorrow that we Christians were depriving ourselves of the pleasures of this life and wasting a lot of good times. I asked him if his cult had warned him of the consequences of living for pleasure, such as diseases, heartbreak, and betrayal resulting from sexual sin or the addiction and utter devastation resulting from alcohol and drugs. I told him that he had been convinced of a lie that had originated directly from Satan, who the Bible calls the father of liars (John 8:44). Regardless of what he was taught, once we leave this life to enter eternity, there is no second chance at repentance. I could only urge him to receive Christ as his Saviour and forsake the teachings of this cult before it was too late.

On another occasion, a group of Muslim imams attended one of our church services and stayed afterward to ask what I thought of Mohammed, the prophet of Islam, and of the Koran. I responded that Mohammed was undoubtedly an intelligent man who founded a simple religion that appealed to many people, but who missed the whole point and knew nothing about God's redemption of mankind. The Koran, I told them, is an amalgamation of verses with no particular theme, no beginning and no ending, and it was written by someone who was clearly intelligent enough to omit any prophecies that would have exposed the document as false. Obviously frustrated with this answer, the men then asked what I thought of Islam, and when I replied there is no salvation in it, they questioned what made me believe the Bible was the true Word of God.

I told them Jesus Christ is the Saviour, the center of our Bible, and the sacrifice offered on the cross for mankind. Then I told them of the biblical prophecies that have been fulfilled down to the letter and of the prophecy that the Jews will return to Israel at the end of days. If they wanted to prove the Bible false, I challenged them to join the Muslim nations in war against Israel and defeat it. Unable to find an argument to my reasoning, they left with much to think about.

Our church conducted a Bible conference every year of the Lebanese War, held in a small hotel in a mountain village in the heart of the Maronite Catholic area. The Lord blessed tremendously as we saw many people come to Christ. Among those who were saved were folks living in the village near the hotel who had heard a conference was in town and attended our meetings out of curiosity. The priest of the village soon came to meet me, obviously seeking to determine what we were about. As we talked over coffee, I learned he was educated in Switzerland and had recently come to Lebanon. When he asked me about my people and what I believed in, I explained we were Christians who believed in the Bible and its literal interpretation.

He asked if I believed in or prayed to Saint Mary, and rather than answering directly, I asked him how Mary became a saint. He then answered that she had become a saint by believing in Jesus and if we believe in Him, we too could become saints. Then I asked him whether he would go to Heaven if he were to die that evening, and his demeanor abruptly turned serious as he told me firmly that no one could be assured of Heaven. I gently corrected him, telling him God gives assurance in the Bible that Heaven is the eternal destination of those who believe. I read to him from 1 John 5:11–13: "And this is the record, that God hath given to us eternal life, and this life is in his Son. He that hath the Son hath life; and he that hath not the Son of God hath not life. These things have I written unto you that believe on the name of the Son of God; that ye may know that ye have eternal life, and that ye may believe on the name of the Son of God."

The priest digested this for a moment, then tossed out another rebuttal, asking if I had heard of the claim of a recent discovery of manuscripts that discredited the Bible and about a supposed lost letter to the church of Laodicea. Rather than argue, I pointed him to the gospels, which he claimed to believe were true: "Heaven and earth shall pass away, but my words shall not pass away" (Matthew 24:35).

I told him that nothing can discredit the Bible because it is the complete Word of God, and any missing letter was not inspired by God. Still unbelieving, although I urged him to settle the matter of his uncertainty about eternity, the priest left to conduct mass for his congregation, promising to come see me the next day. I waited for him the next day and the day after that, but he did not return. After our meeting, I thought often about how many people in that village trusted him to help them get to Heaven, although in reality he knew neither the Saviour nor the way.

In our ministry, we also encountered Jehovah's Witnesses, many of whom sincerely believed the literature of their false doctrine was true and desperately needed by others. Since they also went door to door seeking to evangelize the community, we often met each other in different homes, sometimes resulting in heated conversations.

As we visited one family, a pair of Jehovah's Witnesses also knocked on their door and entered the house to sit with the family and some friends that had gathered with us. It soon became clear that the leader planned to attack our doctrine with difficult questions designed to prove to the family that Jehovah's

Witnesses know the Scripture and can apply the truth, while Christians are ignorant of Scripture and cannot defend our faith.

I recognized the Jehovah's Witness cult as a formidable enemy, differing from other cults in its use of the Scriptures. In those days, they carried a booklet with verses from the Bible twisted in a way to discredit the deity of Christ—which is what one of the men challenged me with as he settled in his seat. When I told him I indeed believed in the deity of Jesus Christ, he asked how I interpreted John 1:18, which says, "No man hath seen God at any time; the only begotten Son, which is in the bosom of the Father, he hath declared him." If no one has seen God but people saw Christ, he posed, how can Christ be God?

I told him I would explain the verse if he could tell me who created the universe. He answered that God created the logos (Jesus Christ), and logos created everything. I asked him to read Isaiah 44:24, in which the prophet wrote, "Thus saith the Lord, thy redeemer, and he that formed thee from the womb, I am the Lord that maketh all things; that stretcheth forth the heavens alone; that spreadeth abroad the earth by myself."

The man was forced to admit the verse declared God alone created everything. This, I told him, was consistent with Genesis 1:1, John 1:3, and Romans 11:33, all of which declare that God is the source of all things. Either the Holy Spirit of God was confused on the matter, or Jehovah's Witnesses and all others who deny the deity of Christ are confused, because Jesus told His disciples He was God: "If ye had known me, ye should have known my Father also: and from henceforth ye know him, and have seen him. Philip saith unto him, Lord, shew us the Father, and it sufficeth us. Jesus saith unto him, Have I been so long time with you, and yet hast thou not known me, Philip? he that hath seen me hath seen the Father; and how sayest thou then, Shew us the Father?" (John 14:7–9).

As everyone in the room listened, I read from Mark 2, in which four men dug through a ceiling to give their palsied friend access to Jesus, and Jesus responded to the man's need not by healing his body, but by forgiving his sins. How could Jesus have forgiven sins, a power only available to God, if He were not God? I explained that Jesus can forgive sins, restore health and life, and save precisely because He is God the Son—God Incarnate.

As powerful and persuasive as the Scripture is, the Jehovah's Witnesses did not accept Christ and His Word that day. They, like so many others, had been blinded to the truth. As evidenced by these few examples, Satan's influence in our community through false teaching, whether in the form of Muslim, Catholic, or Jehovah's Witness, was strong—but we praised the Lord for the victories we did see in the lives of many who were set free and given hope through Jesus Christ.

Ten

TURNING UP THE HEAT

In 1989, the war in Lebanon took a turn for the worse as the Lebanese Christian Forces and the Lebanese Army turned against each other, seriously destabilizing the Christian community. By May 1990, the situation had deteriorated to the point that the imminent clash between these two groups endangered everyone living in East Beirut. Even areas described as safe havens in the past became vulnerable. The roads from our home to our church became extremely dangerous as snipers hid everywhere, shooting indiscriminately at innocent bystanders. My house overflowed with guests desperately trying to escape the hot spots in the city.

But in these increasingly difficult days, God's protection on our family and the believers of our church was distinctly noticeable—not only to us but also to unbelievers around us.

Miraculous Protection

As the violence intensified, one family living in an area called Forn El Shabek was so afraid their home would become the line of demarcation that the teenage children asked to take refuge in our home. We welcomed the entire family gladly, but their parents decided to stay behind so no one would loot or occupy the house. As the battle began, with militias fighting fiercely from one street to another, radio broadcasters regularly announced the name of each street where fighting was taking place. Naturally, the children we sheltered hovered constantly over the set listening for any news of their home and parents. Rosann and I prayed earnestly for their parents' safety, knowing it was quite possible they had been killed. Particularly difficult was the fact that telephone lines and all other forms of communication between our home and theirs were completely cut off. Rosann and I did our best to comfort the children, urging them to trust in the Lord.

These young people were not alone in their fear; the others who had taken refuge in our home during that battle also worried about their families and homes. We had about eleven people staying with us, which made it necessary for me to take many gallon jugs and drive up to the mountain nearly every other day to refill our drinking water supply for our guests. In time, my back began to hurt from carrying jugs of water up the three flights of stairs to our apartment. Even so, I was thankful for the opportunity to be able to provide refuge for and help others in this way.

After several days of intense fighting, we heard on the radio that the Lebanese Christian Army had prevailed against the Lebanese Forces, forcing them to pull out of the Forn El Shabek suburb. Because lines of communication were down, we were not surprised that the teens still could not reach their parents, nor that they were soon desperate to leave our home to search for them and determine whether they had survived the battle. Those who were in the house with us gathered around them and earnestly urged them not to leave, as the teenage boys could easily be mistaken on the street as Lebanese Forces members and kidnapped. But when it became clear the children would not be dissuaded, I decided to risk driving them to their parents' home.

We saw unbelievable destruction around us as we neared Forn El Shabek. Houses lay in ruins with collapsed walls and debris littering the ground in such volume that I had to stop the car some distance away from their house and we walked the rest of the way. Armed military swarmed everywhere around the area as we picked our way through what used to be orderly neighborhood streets and located the teens' home. We were thrilled to find their parents still alive. Their mother told me they had literally stared death in the face, but the hand of the Lord had protected them. The fighting surged all around their high-rise building, yet not one person in it had been harmed. Together, we praised the Lord for His divine protection.

God also mercifully protected another church family that lived in a village that was bombarded almost daily by the Muslim militia and Syrian forces. This was one of our most faithful families, among the first to arrive at church whenever the doors opened, committed to participating in visitation, witnessing, house meetings, and fellowships at our home on Sunday afternoons. Their son even led the singing at our worship services. When the fighting touched down in their area, their neighbors began to notice that though bombs were falling everywhere and hitting many homes, the house of that family was never hit. Additionally, this family neither hid nor became nervous even in the face of heavy fighting. Neighbors asked the family for their secret, and the eldest young man in the house smiled, realizing this was an opportunity to tell his neighbors about Jesus.

Another man in our church, who had been my assistant after attending Bible college, noticed one day that his car's fuel gauge was on empty. Because an impending battle would soon close stores and gas stations, he recognized that he needed to refuel quickly, so he went in search of a gas station that was still open. Finding one, he pulled in and had just begun to pump gas when another car suddenly sped into the station and parked behind him. The driver seemed nervous and urgently pressed his horn to challenge my assistant to hurry. My assistant finished refueling, paid the cashier, and hastened to leave the station—only to hear the explosion of a mortar bomb seconds after he had driven around the corner. The bomb struck the car that had been behind him, killing the driver on impact and setting the gas station on fire.

On yet another occasion, a group of believers were gathered in a home on the top floor of a high-rise building for prayer and Bible study when in the middle of the meeting a cannon bomb suddenly ripped through the ceiling and landed on a coffee table in the living room. The coffee table shattered, but the bomb did not detonate–which was extremely unusual for this type of explosive. Everyone stood in stunned silence for a few seconds, and, before they could gather their wits, another cannon bomb tore a second hole in the ceiling and landed near the first, causing damage to the living room floor but also not detonating. Its arrival jarred the believers back to their senses, and they promptly left everything behind, jerked open the door, and ran down the stairs as fast as they could. By the time they reached the last flight of stairs, a third bomb had struck, and this one detonated, demolishing the entire floor where moments before the Christians had been praying.

Many true believers of Christ in Lebanon have similar stories of divine protection. They too passed through the war and became intimately acquainted with the valley of the shadow of death but were spared by the Lord from harm and death. We were careful to testify of His grace to us so that our children and our community would know the salvation and goodness of the Lord even amid the ravages of war.

At the end of May 1990, the Lebanese Army finally defeated the Lebanese Christian Forces and forced them to retreat farther north of Beirut, which led to the reopening of the roads that led to our church and our guests' houses. While many were able to return to home in relative peace, others remained because their home areas were still very dangerous. The gas stations and many food stores remained closed, so I continued to store fuel for my car in our guest bathroom and bags of rice and flour throughout the house to sustain ourselves and any who took refuge with us. Together, we kept watchful eyes and ears on the news and prepared for what was to come next.

A Temporary Goodbye

As anyone familiar with world events during the late 1980s and early 1990s will know, this period was rife with conflict for both the Middle East and the world as a whole. In 1988, Saddam Hussein declared victory over Iran after Khomeini agreed to a cease fire. The price of victory, however, was high—tremendous destruction in both countries and casualties in the millions. And while the year 1989 marked the historic fall of the Berlin Wall, the toppling of Communism did nothing to distract Saddam Hussein, whose ultimate objective was to invade and destroy Israel, from turning his attention toward Kuwait. He told the Kuwaitis they owed him an enormous sum for his protection against Iran. When the Kuwaiti government refused to pay, insisting it owed nothing because Hussein started the war, he prepared to attack, an action that would hasten a global-scale conflict just months later.

Meanwhile in Lebanon, the summer of 1990 brought a significant shift in the military powers fighting in the country. Not only did the Lebanese Christian Army solidify its control over a large part of Beirut, but on the Muslim side there were also major battles between the pro-Syrian militias and those supported by Yasser Arafat and the PLO. With help from the Syrian Army, the pro-Syrian militias defeated the PLO, driving Yasser Arafat and his militias from Beirut to the northern city of Tripoli and its surrounding suburbs. By June, the Palestinian bases and all of West Beirut were under the total control of the Syrian Army.

Because of the unrest, we often had no electricity and relied on candles for light, and we rationed our fuel, putting just enough in our car tank to make it to church and back for fear it would be siphoned by night thieves. Rosann and some of the ladies in our church made homemade bread with the flour we stored, and we ate it with whatever food was available. But as the weeks wore on with no means of replenishing our supplies, we began to run out. By the middle of June I realized that for my family's safety, our time in Lebanon, at least for the present, had come to an end.

I asked Rosann to start packing while I made our travel arrangements: boat passage from North Beirut into Cyprus, and airfare from Cyprus to the United States. I left some money with the people living in our home to buy food should the stores re-open, then drove my family to the seaport for an evening departure. We were told our boat would leave at 7:00 or 8:00 that evening, but hundreds of people had also booked passage, wanting to escape Lebanon, so it was near midnight before we were finally on our way.

Our watercraft was a hovermatic boat that hovered over the water, propelled by huge fans. Because of the danger represented by the fighting around us, the boat dared not show any lights, and the captain instructed everyone on board to abstain from turning on lights of any kind as well. The boat rose on a column of air and hovered away from the shore and into the dark expanse of the Mediterranean Sea to avoid being seen and potentially fired upon by Syrian forces encamped in the nearby hillsides. After traveling cautiously for half an hour, the crew judged we were far enough away from danger to turn the lights on, and we continued moving slowly through the night.

We arrived at Cyprus early the next morning and boarded our flight to the United States. It was an easy flight and enjoyable for the children and Rosann, but it was not as easy for me. Deep in my heart, I realized although we had planned this to be a temporary escape from Lebanon, I could not knowingly endanger my wife and children by returning with them. I might have to return to Lebanon by myself while they remained in America where they would be safe. I refrained from speaking of this; I did not want to alarm my family about my feelings or my intentions until we had safely arrived and things had settled down.

Southside Baptist Church, our sending church in Greenville, South Carolina, was thrilled to see us back safely. They helped us purchase furniture for the apartment we rented and helped us establish ourselves once more in America. I thanked the Lord for our church family because their efforts provided me great physical and psychological relief—which I desperately needed. By this time, I was experiencing sharp pains in my back that were being referred to my chest, making me fear I was about to have a heart attack. After a few tests and an exam by a skilled doctor, however, I learned the problem was much less serious than I feared—I had displaced two vertebrae from all those trips carrying five-gallon jugs of water up three flights of stairs to replenish our supplies in Lebanon. A quick massage and adjustment later, I was pain-free.

The days following our arrival were wonderful. We found a used car and were able to visit a few of our supporting churches to give reports on what God was doing in Lebanon. Our children enjoyed going to places they could not go in Lebanon, such as McDonald's, Burger King, and the Dollar Store; and Rosann and I enjoyed the freedom to take family walks around the lake at our apartment complex and watch our children chase the ducks nearby without fear of falling bombs or sniper fire. Our friends at Southside Baptist Church went out of their way to make us feel welcomed and comfortable. Many invited us to dinner in their homes or took us to local restaurants. Rosann's mother came down from New York to see us and the children. Altogether, this much-needed loving care took our minds off the tension in the Persian Gulf and Lebanon.

After a few weeks, when my family had settled in again, I told Rosann of my intention to return to continue the ministry in Lebanon. I reasoned that many people work in other countries and leave their families behind for a time, and the time would surely pass quickly, having only a small effect on our family.

When he heard of my plan to leave, Dr. Handford, our pastor at Southside Baptist, joined other members in expressing deep concern for my safety. He did not think it necessary for me to minister in such a dangerous situation and was afraid I would be injured or killed if I returned. I explained that if I did not return, the ministry in Lebanon would suffer. Furthermore, I told him I did not believe God would send me to Lebanon and allow me to die before I finished my job, and since He called me there, He would go before me to protect me.

Dr. Handford realized he could not dissuade me from returning, so he assured me the congregation of Southside Baptist would take care of Rosann and my children in my absence and in the event of my death. With this reassurance, I set about making arrangements to return to the field, and all too soon the time came to board my flight back to Cyprus. As the plane lifted off and I watched the shores of America grow smaller in the distance, I had no idea that the days ahead would be some of the hardest of my life.

In our absence, tensions in the Middle East had escalated beyond description. In August of 1990, the Iraqi Army invaded Kuwait and literally looted the country, killing and imprisoning many Kuwaitis. The invasion created a great stir both in the Middle East and around the globe. Fearing Saddam Hussein might attempt to occupy the Arabian Peninsula and control the majority of the world's oil, the United States and other world powers moved against him, amassing their forces in the Saudi Arabian desert for Operation Desert Shield.

As for Lebanon, the country had reflected the Middle Eastern tension and was a virtual time bomb on the brink of explosion. On landing at the seaport north of Beirut, although I was assured by the brethren awaiting my arrival that I would be relatively safe, I immediately sensed nervousness in the air. Before long, my nervousness turned to unrest as the Syrian armies invaded East Beirut in October and defeated the Christian Lebanese Army. Thousands of bombs flew in all directions throughout the city, damaging homes and killing many innocent people. Due to the intensified fighting, General Aoun, head of the Lebanese army, fled to the French Embassy while most of the Lebanese army simply ran or surrendered to the Syrian forces.

In the midst of all this, the Lord blessed the work in Lebanon tremendously. Our home Bible studies continued as we knocked on hundreds of doors to tell people about the saving grace of the Lord Jesus Christ. Many approached me to ask if this was the end of the days and whether Jesus was going to come soon. Their fear opened many doors of opportunity to present the plan of salvation and invite people to the Bible conferences we held several times that fall. Between these conferences and the Christian weddings and funerals we held, we rejoiced at many people coming to salvation. That year we baptized twenty-three people, one of whom pastors the church there today. We were also able to start a home Bible study on Friday nights in the home of a man in our church who received Christ during this time.

December of 1990 arrived quickly, bringing with it my desire to spend Christmas and the New Year with my family. While God blessed the ministry and my work in Lebanon and my days were full and busy, my nights were terribly lonely. I desperately missed Rosann, Mitchell, and Julie. Of course, the Lebanon believers understood my need to be reunited with my family, and my assistant agreed to fill the pulpit in my absence.

My family and some dear friends met me at the airport in South Carolina for a joyful reunion. As I arrived at our apartment, I discovered a new addition to our family—a cocker spaniel named Buffy. I was pleased my family now had the protection of a dog—although of course, Buffy had to adjust to me and learn in time that I was the head of the family, and not she.

We spent a wonderful Christmas and New Year together, and a few days after the New Year, Pastor Handford asked me to preach for the January 16 Wednesday night service. He suggested I explain to the church what was going on in Iraq and the Middle East. By Wednesday night, the word had spread that I was preaching on the Middle East, and many folks came. As the rest of the congregation sang praise and worship to the Lord, I sat with my notes and my Bible, prayerfully reviewing and preparing for the message. Just before I stood to preach, a man drew Pastor Handford aside and whispered something to him. With a worried expression, the pastor addressed the church a moment later to announce that the Gulf War had just begun. The American military and its allies were moving toward Kuwait to confront the Iraqi Army that occupied the country.

I was just as stunned by the news as everyone else, and I realized the congregations would naturally be distracted as I preached, so I paused to pray God would give my words power enough to hold their attention. That night I preached a sermon the Lord had prepared in my heart many months before entitled, "America and Iraq in the Bible." I encouraged the people to open their Bibles to Jeremiah 49–50 and showed them how the Bible mentions Iraq and the Gulf War, quoting the verses that point to Saddam Hussein as the modern-day Nebuchadnezzar. Finally, I turned to Isaiah 13 and showed them that America is mentioned in the Bible and that Saddam Hussein would be defeated, demonstrating that his kingdom was going to be destroyed.

I have preached thousands of sermons in my life but none so timely as the sermon I preached that night. The Lord used it in my life and the lives of those in the congregation to ease fears and establish confidence in His Word and plan.

All too soon, my Christmas vacation was over, and I was on my way back to the ministry in Lebanon. The country I was returning to was as dark and dangerous as I had left it, as it was still fully under Syrian control. But there was hope—the victory of America and her allies over Saddam Hussein's armies stabilized the Middle East, creating a relative calm and opening new doors for ministry.

Eleven

A NEW DOOR OPENS

I have set before thee an open door, and
no man can shut it.—**Revelation 3:8**

In May of 1992, Rosann contacted me and told me the children's school was over for the year, and since there was now relative stability in Lebanon, it was finally time for our family to be reunited. We made the necessary arrangements, and I traveled by boat to meet their plane as it landed in Limosol, Cyprus. As Rosann, the children, and our dog emerged from the plane, my heart nearly burst with joy. I hugged my wife and children tightly, and all the pain and the loneliness I had experienced during the many months without them were forgotten. Together we traveled back to Lebanon, where many of our church family were waiting to welcome them back.

But what did it mean to be "back"? Over the next few years, I struggled with the decision of what would be the next step in the ministry to which the Lord had called me. The church was doing well by this time, and we had seen many people saved. The question that constantly challenged me was: "As a missionary, should I stay and pastor Bible Baptist Church, or should I move on and plant other churches?" I knew staying would mean being a pastor and no longer truly a missionary, as I believe a missionary's calling is to evangelize people, establish a local indigenous church, and then move on and repeat the process. But the opportunities to serve as a missionary were dwindling rapidly during this period. Arab and Muslim nations began to close their doors to foreign missionaries, which meant that foreigners could no longer enter countries as missionaries and openly evangelize. They could live as tourists and attend English or international community churches but could not openly establish new national churches.

A Larger Field

I believed that God had called me to missions, so I prayed He would lead me to wherever He wanted me next. Considering it had taken about ten years to plant the Bible Baptist Church in Beirut, I also prayed the Lord would allow me to plant many more churches in a faster period of time. Through a season of prayer, I believed the Lord was directing me to minister, not just in Lebanon, but across the Middle East, beginning in Egypt.

I felt confident that the Bible Baptist Church in Beirut was ready to function without my leadership. By 1995, the church was completely renovated. We had purchased an adjacent piece of property and converted it into a parking lot and playground. We had also received 35,000 New Testaments, church pews to replace the old termite-infested ones, a new pulpit, and other equipment including a sound system and a Lord's Supper table. The church was truly ready for coming peace in Lebanon.

In preparations to set up the church for our departure, I ordained a young man who had grown under our ministry and delivered the shepherding of the church to him. Confident the body of believers was in good hands, my family and I left for Cairo in pursuit of the vision and call God had given me.

In Egypt, we met many Christians who sincerely loved the Lord, and we ministered for a time in six different cities, teaching the Word of God in different homes. During our stay, the Lord showed me the difficulties His people were experiencing. Christians had developed great fear because of Muslim threats and persecution. Even the Egyptian government, under Hosni Mubarak, had forbidden Christians to build churches or serve the Lord freely. My impression was that in general the Egyptian population was peaceful, but within the Islamic community there was an extreme element that believed Christians (infidels) must be converted to Islam. Muslims targeted Christian women, kidnapping and marrying them and forcibly converting them to Islam. In the rural areas of Egypt, churches were frequently attacked, and Christian weddings were often disrupted. The Egyptian police did nothing to stop this persecution; in fact, the police actually became heavy handed with the church as well. As a result, Christians had no legal recourse or refuge and became strangers in their own country.

I had never seen anything like this happening in Lebanon. Though Lebanese Muslims were religious, they were not fanatic, and while Christians and Muslims argued over political issues, they respected each other's holidays. But in Egypt, I found myself exposed to something deeply disturbing that I had not before experienced. Stirred by their suffering, I spent a whole year encouraging the Egyptian believers in Christ, urging them not to give up.

One day, I was invited to minister to a very large church in downtown Cairo. I preached on the four names of God that do not exist in Islam: God is Love, our Saviour, our Father, and our hope. (The God of Islam has ninety-nine character names; however, these four names of God are not among them.) I explained it was the love of God that led Him to provide salvation for us, and when we are saved, we become His children and can address Him as "Our Father." Moreover, because our Heavenly Father has given us eternal life through the sacrifice of our Lord Jesus, we are children of hope. I illustrated that Jesus Christ, God the Son, is the member of the trinity who is active in the history of mankind. I showed them that the God who walked with Adam and Eve, appeared to Enoch and Abraham, and walked with Shadrach, Meshach, and Abednego in the fiery furnace is the same God who took on human flesh, was born of the virgin Mary, and offered Himself as sacrifice on the cross for our sins. I concluded with a benediction: "To Him, Jesus, be the honor, glory, worship, and praise forever and ever." At these words, the people in the sanctuary began to shout with loud voices, giving honor and glory to the Lord Jesus Christ. Their voices were so loud that the whole neighborhood could hear. My heart was moved at their response, and I resolved to continue ministering to Christians and planting churches throughout the Muslim world.

The Heathen for an Inheritance

Very soon afterward, the Lord showed me it was time for us to leave Egypt. After a time of prayer, we decided to continue on to Detroit, Michigan, where we knew there was a large population of Arabic people. The Lord enabled us to minister to many through a local Arabic church and blessed us with many good friends. Among them was Brother Saber, an American Iraqi believer and a businessman who partnered with me in reaching and witnessing to countless Arabic-speaking families.

All along I knew that our stay in Michigan was temporary and that we were simply there to pursue the Lord's will and His direction for our next steps. During that period many churches stood behind us, praying for and supporting us. Then one night, as I was in my bedroom reading in the book of Psalms, the Lord spoke to me through a particular verse: "Ask of me, and I shall give thee the heathen for thine inheritance, and the uttermost parts of the earth for thy possession" (Psalm 2:8).

I told the Lord that those who live in the Arab world are heathen, Gentiles, the children of Ishmael and the anti-type of Isaac. Yet John 3:16 tells us that God so loved the world, and the Middle East is part of that world. I asked Him to give me the Middle East for His glory. I told Him that as I know the Arabic language, culture, and people, I was available to be used by Him for these people.

In answer, the Lord showed me through 2 Timothy 2:2 that if I could find faithful men, train them, and stand behind them, they would be able to reach their own nations with the gospel. Although foreign missionaries may not be able to minister in certain countries because of the inherent danger to their lives and the lives of others, nationals can serve the Lord effectively because they already speak the language and share the culture of the land. Furthermore, people trust them more readily, and in case of political disruption, they may not need to flee the country. Additionally, they do not need the large sum of money required to sustain a foreign missionary.

Two days later, Brother Saber phoned me to tell me about some Arab refugees, a majority of them Iraqi, who were living in Greece. He asked if I would be interested in going to Greece with him to preach for a revival there. My answer was an enthusiastic, "Yes!" I praised the Lord for providing a partner in the ministry. Thus, in 1996 we traveled together to Greece to preach revival, and we saw hundreds of people come to Christ. While there, we contacted a church in Athens known to host Arabic people and asked the pastor to invite them to attend a series of evening revival meetings. When we arrived, we were delighted to discover everyone was waiting for us in anticipation of what the Lord would do. Each night, I gave an invitation for salvation following my message, and each night I was greatly encouraged by the large numbers of people who came forward to give their lives to the Lord. It seemed people were coming from everywhere just to hear the gospel.

In Athens we heard there were large numbers of Arabic refugees in Istanbul, Turkey, so we headed there to conduct more evangelistic meetings. When we arrived, we found people suffering from loneliness and confusion, many of whom seemed to have little idea what direction their lives should take after the disruptions of war and unrest. They had to settle for meager jobs while seeking asylum in the West, and many realized their homeland was closed, and they had no hope of returning. While their plight was terrible, it gave us a wonderful opportunity. Many were now open to hearing of the hope found in Jesus, whereas before their distress, they would never have taken the time to listen.

When we planned the meetings, I was unsure how many might attend, considering the oppressive atmosphere in the city. The Arabs in Istanbul were accustomed to meeting in a foreign embassy and walking in very small groups for fear of harassment by the secret police. When Brother Saber and I arrived in Istanbul, we were instructed to carry our passports at all times and to avoid walking in large groups. On our first Sunday in Istanbul, the meeting began with just a few people. By the time I stood to preach, however, the hall was packed. Somehow people had managed to come from all across the city to hear God's Word. And as in Greece, when I gave the invitation, many people came to receive Christ as their Saviour.

One of the men with whom I prayed that Sunday joyfully declared that it was the best day of his life. He then told me he believed Saddam Hussein was the greatest evangelist the world had ever known. At my shocked reaction, he explained further. He told me how greatly he had suffered in escaping from Iraq: beaten, tortured, and nearly killed in Kurdistan by Kurdish rebels, and treated even worse at the hands of the Turks. When I responded that it seemed all his troubles were actually because of Saddam Hussein, he corrected me. He told me it was the foolishness and evil of Saddam that had driven him to leave Iraq and escape to Turkey, where he had heard about this revival meeting and where the Lord had touched his heart and saved him. "So," he concluded with a smile, "thanks to Saddam Hussein, I'm a now born-again Christian!" That simple statement deeply touched my heart as I was reminded that God's way is always perfect.

A New Continent

The next year, 1997, the Lord opened a door for me to visit some African believers who had been saved in our ministry in Lebanon and were now ministering in Kumasi, the second largest city in Ghana. This was an answer to the call and the burden on my life to help train faithful men. I traveled to Kumasi to help the brethren start a church. When I arrived, I could not help but notice the area was already represented by churches of many denominations. I asked Brother Peter Mensah, who became the pastor of the new church, why we needed yet another church in Ghana. He told me the Ghanians needed churches that did not cater to their emotions but to their spiritual needs. I understood what he meant when I later discovered many Ghanians were interested in spiritual matters but wanted little personal responsibility for their spiritual growth. Instead of reading, studying, and meditating on the Word of God, they preferred churches that provided excitement, encouraging them to jump and shout, and they favored pastors who taught that giving money to God would ensure prosperity and good health (a teaching many American ministries also endorse). The Ghanians desperately needed a church that taught God's Word and stood for the truth without compromise or apology.

We began planting that church. For two years, we met in a school, but after the school was destroyed by a storm, we prayed earnestly and were able to raise enough money to purchase property on which to construct a church building seating about five hundred people. The new church building drew much attention, even from the media, with more than seven hundred people attending the dedication service. With time, the ministry grew as people were saved and obeyed the Lord in baptism. Later, we also started a Bible institute so that pastors from around Kumasi could study the Word of God.

The news of our church's growth spread throughout West Africa and was heard by pastors from Togo, who then traveled to Kumasi to ask me to come to their country and help them as well. Not long after, I was headed to Togo with a group of Bible teachers from the States to conduct Bible conferences and seminars. There, just as in Kumasi, we saw many people saved and several men ordained to the ministry.

During these years in Africa, I often returned home, which by now was in Knoxville, Tennessee. One day while there, I received a call from an African man I knew well who told me of an African leader, John Demey, who had spent his life serving the Lord as the pastor of a large church in Liberia. Many men had gone out from his church to plant daughter churches all throughout the country. Pastor Demey was traveling in the States and had heard about me, and he wanted to visit me. I was glad to meet him, and I found him to be an honorable man with a remarkable story. As a little boy he had never seen a white man until missionaries came and led him and many others to the Lord. Sadly, his experience following salvation was anything but encouraging to a young Christian. The missionaries discriminated against the African people in that town, and while they enjoyed electricity and air conditioning, they denied these luxuries to the nationals, even prohibiting them from drawing close to their lights at night or drinking their water.

Pastor Demey related that when the civil war had broken out in Liberia, the missionaries simply abandoned their compounds, leaving their SUVs and small planes behind, and neglected to send so much as a penny or a loaf of bread from America to help support the nationals. They left these Liberian believers to their destiny, which was likely to be death at the hands of the rebels, while they returned to America to tell the churches of their own suffering. And when the Liberian national pastors contacted the mission board to ask for help, they received no response. One of Brother Demey's assistants subsequently found the bylaws of that mission board, and they were shocked to discover in them the mission board's policy that missionaries were not to give assistance to any national.

What a blow this must have been to the national churches. Nonetheless, with civil war once again raging in Liberia, Brother Demey quietly appealed to me for help. I told him the war would complicate any effort I might make there, but I promised him I would pray and seek wisdom from the Lord before I gave him my answer. When I approached the Lord about the matter, He reminded me I had gone through the war of Lebanon unafraid. Why should civil war in Liberia scare me? So I told Brother Demey I would return with him to Liberia. At the time, however, he was in America to undergo medical tests. When his doctors informed him he had cancer and advised him to remain in the States, it became necessary for me to plan the trip to Liberia without him.

As I was making preparations for the trip, a veteran missionary called to warn me against dealing with nationals. He explained they could not be trusted and had no knowledge of how to handle money. Not wishing to ignore a sincere warning, I prayerfully considered his words; ultimately, however, I concluded if missionaries felt they could not trust the nationals, it was because they never taught them responsibility. These African brothers needed someone to trust them and teach them leadership, and I determined to be that person. With this charge ahead of me, and with a few men who agreed to make the journey alongside me, I traveled to Liberia and met Pastor Demey's son and many other pastors. They were thrilled and encouraged to know that we were willing to take such a risk to come to their country. Later, I received a poignant letter from the national pastors telling me our visit filled their hearts with joy and proved to them there were still people who loved and cared for them.

How the Lord blessed us in Liberia! We showed the nationals we were willing to trust them, and in return they proved to us they could be accountable. The Lord gave us a radio station, high schools, a Bible college, and a refuge center for those who come from a non-Christian background. The churches in Ghana, Togo, and Liberia are still going strong, and the believers there continue to faithfully serve the Lord.

God used this time in Africa, just as in Greece and Turkey, to show me He has raised up faithful men in every country who are willing and able to reach their nations with the gospel and become valued partners in the ministry. As we were faithful to follow His call to these nations, God greatly enlarged our ministry. Today, it covers six major Arab countries and three West African countries with open doors in many more. To God be the glory for the great things He has done and will do in these countries in the future.

Miracles in Iraq

In my life and ministry, I have learned the Lord directs us to the place of His will by three different methods. First, He leads us as we diligently read and study the Bible. Second, God uses circumstances in our lives to confirm His will to us. Third, the Holy Spirit, using the Word of God and sometimes the counsel of others, guides us to His will by giving us inner peace about a particular direction for our lives.

After the attack of September 11, 2001, the United States' presence in the Middle East was stronger than ever. In January and February of 2003, the American military and their allies prepared to invade Iraq in Operation Iraqi Freedom in a battle Saddam Hussein described as the "Mother of All Battles." At the time, Rosann and I were in Florida staying in a mission house when a friend of ours, the son of a prominent Baptist leader, visited us. He told us Iraq was about to be opened to the gospel and asked if I would be interested in going there with him.

Of course I was interested, but I explained to him that opening a country to the initial presentation of the gospel would require much preliminary planning. Nothing could be done quickly. We would have to look for people who shared our faith, and it was not always easy to find someone faithful, honest, and willing to serve the Lord wholeheartedly.

The young man was undeterred. His idea was to simply plant a church in Baghdad and quickly move on to something else. Though we certainly did not see eye-to-eye on church planting in an Arabic country, what was clear was the country of Iraq was indeed about to open. Soon there would be a small window of opportunity for me to plant a church there, and I determined to go to Iraq as soon as was practical. I prayed earnestly to the Lord and put the matter in His hands, knowing that His calling is His enabling.

In March 2003, the invasion of Iraq began with great American successes. The American military and her allies swiftly defeated the Iraqi army and captured Saddam Hussein. By the end of May, the American news media was reporting its military had removed the land mines from most of the roads leading to Baghdad. To me, this meant the time had come.

I called Brother Saber and told him about my burden to plant a church in Baghdad. He immediately agreed to accompany me on the trip, so soon after we flew to Beirut and from there attempted to go by land, through Syria, to Iraq. The Syrian authorities would not allow Brother Saber to cross their border because he was Iraqi by birth. So we changed plans and flew from Beirut to Amman, the capital of Jordan. There, we were thrilled to discover Americans did not need a visa to enter Iraq, so we hired a taxi to drive us the fourteen hours to Baghdad.

The drive from Amman to Baghdad was a unique experience for me. The trip was naturally fraught with tension because we were going into unknown territory. Furthermore, we would be entering a war zone, though that was not unfamiliar to me. Perhaps it was just memories that unsettled me as we drove. At the Jordanian border we waited in a seemingly endless line of cars behind a myriad of people who were desperately trying to leave Jordan and return to their homeland. Long caravans of trucks carried commodities. We handed our passports to the border security forces and stood in line for two hours waiting for our names to be called before we were allowed to cross the border into Iraq.

The first thing I saw when we entered Iraq was an abundance of U.S. military forces. As they checked our passports, I was struck by how young most of them were—some as young as my own son. I resisted the urge to reach out and hug them. They were so kind and polite, and we did all we could to give them encouragement, expressing our gratitude for setting the Iraqi people free. As we pulled away, I glanced out the taxi window to notice some of the young servicemen sitting by the side of the road reading their Bibles. A couple blocks further was another group of soldiers sitting in a circle with their Bibles and obviously praying, and I was deeply touched.

The road to Baghdad was long but well paved. On the sides of the road, we saw Iraqi tanks, trucks, and other military equipment completely destroyed, reflections of the intensity of the fighting and the might and precision of the American military. I spent much of my time during the drive in silent prayer, imploring the Lord to provide a man in Baghdad after His own heart, a man called by Him to start a church, and a man I could train and work together with to minister in Iraq.

When we arrived in Baghdad, I discovered the most prominent evangelical church was the Presbyterian church. When the Presbyterian minister heard that a preacher was in town, he invited me to come and preach in his church. Normally, I would only preach in Baptist churches, but Brother Saber earnestly encouraged me to accept the invitation, preach an evangelistic sermon, and give a closing invitation. So the next Sunday afternoon, I preached to a church filled with worshippers who had come to hear one who had come all the way to Baghdad from America. To my great surprise, a large number of people raised their hands when I gave an invitation for salvation—among them the pastor's own daughter. This encouraging response served to assure me the Lord would indeed bless our ministry in Iraq.

After the service, a man told me the following day there would be a prayer meeting led by a man named Maher Daoud. I had already heard much about this man, so I decided to attend the meeting. The next day I listened to Maher speak of the need for planting churches so the Iraqis could hear about the Saviour. I approached him after the service and shared my vision with him, and he became visibly excited, explaining that he had been praying for years the Lord would bring a man like me to help them start churches. As we continued talking, I recognized this was the man for whom I had been praying.

Maher and I immediately began looking for a house to rent to hold services in, but no matter how many we viewed, something always seemed to be wrong. Either the house was too small, or it was in a bad neighborhood, or the rent was so high we could not afford it. Three months later we were still looking and growing discouraged, even more so as I realized I was due to leave for the States very soon.

With only a few days before my departure, I awoke at 5:00 in the morning with a burdened heart. In near desperation, I asked the Lord to help us find something within the next two days. Three hours later, Maher rushed to my hotel to tell me God had awakened him at 5:00 that morning with the name of a Christian man who owned a house in Baghdad but was living in California. Excitedly, we called this man, and he agreed to rent us his house at an affordable monthly rate for our ministry. The moment we saw the house, we realized God had answered our prayers. It was in just the right area, and it only needed a few small renovations and rearrangements of the rooms to make it serviceable for a church.

I flew back to the States with a heart full of praise. I knew the Lord had answered our prayers and was going to bless us. Brother Maher led the way with the renovations in my absence, and the process took only two months to complete. On November 2, 2003, the New Testament Baptist Church of Baghdad met for the first time. Seven people attended the first service, but it soon began to grow. According to Pastor Maher, it was the first Baptist church of any kind to officially assemble in the country of Iraq, so I felt it should be publicly inaugurated. We appointed January 9, 2004, for the dedication of the church, and close to that date, several preachers from America, a few pastors from the Middle East, and I met in Amman to travel to Baghdad and attend the inaugural service.

Instead of traveling by land as Brother Saber and I had done, we flew to Baghdad on a small plane. Because the Iraqi insurgents possessed anti-aircraft missiles, the American military had cleared a wide area around the airport as the safety zone. In order to avoid anti-aircraft missiles, when our plane approached Baghdad, it suddenly climbed to a very high altitude and maintained it until just above the airport. It then executed a steep nosedive and spiraled down in hopes of a safe landing. We were not warned ahead of time, and we had no idea what was happening. Some of the passengers thought the pilots had lost control, and we were about to crash. One passenger even vomited on the person in front of him. I was actually glad we had no warning about this maneuver, for we would have been frightened the whole flight instead of only those last few terrifying moments. Nonetheless, when we landed we all thanked the Lord we had survived.

When we arrived at the church, Pastor Maher and the church members brought beds into rooms of the church for us to sleep. Some of the American preachers asked to stay in a nearby hotel, but I felt it would be wiser to remain together, so I insisted we all stay in the church. (Little did I realize then, but it was the Lord who placed that burden on my heart. The very next day, insurgents' rockets targeted the hotel where my friends had wanted to stay.) Every day, we awoke early and met in the sanctuary for prayer, then ate a delicious breakfast prepared by some of the church ladies. Afterward, we typically sat in the garden, drank Iraqi tea (very strong and sweet), and enjoyed fellowship with our Iraqi brethren.

The day before the dedication, a stranger came looking for me. He had heard a man named Edgar Feghaly was in town, and he wanted to talk to him. As we talked, he told me he used to be a high-ranking officer in the Iraqi army. I noticed he was carrying a book in Arabic entitled *Muhammad and Jesus*. When I asked about it, he told me he had given it to his imam, who had first ridiculed the book and then gathered his congregation and attacked Jesus and Christianity and the Christian faith.

My visitor explained that he had come to see me so he could ask for my response to things this imam had said. He recounted the imam had said Jesus Christ was a cowardly leader who taught cowardly followers to turn the other cheek, love their enemies, and bless those who curse them. On the contrary, the Koran taught its followers to fight their enemies. Furthermore, the imam had accused Christians of being arrogant cowards because they crucified God and claimed to be able to enter Heaven without doing anything.

When he asked what I had to say against the allegations, I asked him what would be the natural human reaction to someone who caused him great harm, and he answered it was revenge, which was allowed by the Koran. I told him revenge requires no courage, but forgiveness does because it goes against our natural human response. Thus, when Christ taught us to forgive our enemies, He was not teaching cowardice but courage, because mercy and forgiveness are superior to revenge. I then emphasized Matthew 26:52b, in which Jesus said, "for all they that take the sword shall perish with the sword." Saddam

Hussein was a perfect illustration, as he had staged a coup against and killed the previous president, then killed many of his own people, and was then in hiding for fear of being captured and killed himself.

I continued to explain that Christians did not crucify God; in fact, no one could crucify God because God is almighty. God chose to be crucified, and no one could stop Him. Furthermore, I asked him who was more arrogant—the person who prayed thus:

> "God, I thank you because I pray five times a day, fast the month of Ramadan, pay alms to the poor, and I went to the Pilgrimage as you instructed me. I believe in you, your book, and your prophet. I have done everything you asked me to do, and therefore, I deserve the Paradise."

Or the person who prayed thus:

> "God, I'm a sinful person with no hope of redemption apart from you. I don't deserve your kindness and love. Rather, I deserve to go to Hell. I throw myself upon your mercy and beg you to forgive my sins."

The former general seemed stunned. No one had ever answered him this way before. The other preachers joined me in the garden to witness to this man, and before long he knelt down, prayed, and invited the Lord Jesus into his heart. His heart was filled with joy when he left, and he later returned and asked me to witness to his wife and children. I took two of our Middle East pastors to his home, and we led his wife and children to the Lord. The salvation of this man and his family was a great encouragement to us, setting the stage perfectly for the day of the church's dedication.

On January 9, 2004, more than three hundred people came to celebrate the dedication of the New Testament Baptist Church of Baghdad. More people stood outside than inside. Even many Muslims from the vicinity attended the service and rejoiced with us. The spirit of joy and celebration overwhelmed the people. The service was so successful that we decided to follow it with three nights of evangelistic meetings.

The first night when I preached and gave an invitation, about 50 people stood for salvation. Surprised at the high number, I asked them to sit down and explained the plan of salvation again, thinking perhaps they had not fully understood what I was asking them to do. Once more, I gave the invitation, and the same 50 people stood up, so I led them in a sinner's prayer, and they invited the Lord Jesus into their hearts. By the end of the third day, 160 people had given their lives to the Lord.

The church continued to grow, and in 2005, the Lord gave us a miracle. At the suggestion of an American friend, we applied for a radio station license in Baghdad, although we seriously doubted the Islamic government would allow a Christian radio station to operate. The Lord answered our prayers, however, and after one and a half years, the government allocated FM 102.9 for us on May 2, 2006. It was the first Christian radio station licensed by an Islamic government not only in Iraq but also in all the Middle East.

On Christmas Day 2006, we received another miracle. I had frequently traveled to Baghdad to preach at the new church since its inception. Usually toward the end of the services, mothers would bring their children to me and ask me to pray for them because they were afraid of the dark. It was not an uncommon fear; even today, Iraq is able to generate only three hours of electricity daily, so the children spend most of their nights in darkness. At these requests, I would bend down to the children's eye level, put my arms around them, and remind each one that even though we cannot see in the dark, our Lord Jesus can. Furthermore, I reminded them that Jesus loves the little children, and He would send His guardian angels to protect them. Then I prayed with them, remembering that I was just seven years old when I was saved and realizing the presence of the Lord removes children's fears.

As I looked into the faces of the children, I saw how sad they were. The Lord burdened my heart to do something to make them smile. Since 2003, the Lord has enabled me to raise about $500 a year to send to our pastor in Baghdad to purchase Christmas gifts and candy for the children of the church. Quite often the money was provided as the Lord moved American Sunday school and Vacation Bible school children to give generously, and we would tell the Iraqi children this was because the American children loved them and were praying for them.

In 2006, the Lord once more provided the $500, which I sent to Pastor Maher in Baghdad to buy Christmas gifts for the children. He asked if he could use the money for clothing rather than toys or candy because the children did not have adequate clothing. Although I would have preferred they receive toys, I knew the need for clothes was more important. I agreed Brother

Maher should purchase clothes, but I asked that he still wrap them so the children would have gifts to open on Christmas.

That Christmas Day, the church van and bus were bringing the children to church for the Christmas celebration, with Pastor Maher driving the bus. As they neared the church, the pastor noticed the whole area was blocked off by American Marines, who were stopping every car and checking the identity of each driver. When the Marines asked where Pastor Maher was headed, he answered he was going to the local independent Baptist church. After expressing surprise that a Baptist church was nearby, the officer asked if he could accompany Pastor Maher to see it. The pastor consented, and the officer promptly boarded the bus.

At the church, the Marine saw the Christmas tree with gifts under it as Pastor Maher started the electric generator and turned on the lights. The pastor explained they were planning to celebrate Christmas by telling the children and their families the story of the birth of Christ and then distributing the gifts. Then he asked why the Marines were blocking the area. The officer answered that they were very fortunate and must be loved by God because just four houses away from the church building, Marines had found trucks loaded with about twenty tons of explosives. Had the explosives been detonated, the whole area would have been flattened, and the church members would all have been killed. Furthermore, when the Marines found out there was a Baptist church in the area, some of them disappeared for a time and then returned carrying large bags filled with toys and candy for the Christmas tree.

The Lord used another miracle to bring a young Iraqi military officer to salvation. One day this young man was driving near our church when he heard music and singing from one of our services. He parked his jeep and ventured inside the church out of curiosity, but he ended up staying through the end of the service. Afterward, our pastor and several men of the church welcomed him, and the pastor presented him with a small New Testament. He was flattered by the gift and promised to read it.

The next day, he was following through on his promise when he received the call to prepare for battle against a group of insurgents. He ordered his men to get ready, slipped the New Testament into his shirt pocket, and put on his bulletproof vest. The battle was vicious, and in the commotion, the officer took a shot to the chest by an enemy's AK-47 rifle. The bullet struck him squarely over his heart, knocking him to the ground but not killing him. After the battle, as he and his soldiers were returning to their base, the young man took off his vest to find the bullet had penetrated the vest but had been stopped by the New Testament in his shirt pocket. He began to shout in joyful disbelief that the Jesus of the Christians had saved his life. Then he called the church and made an appointment to see Pastor Maher, who sat down with him and showed him how he could become a Christian. Both men knelt and prayed as the young Iraqi officer gave his life to the Lord Jesus Christ.

When they learned of his salvation, this man's wife and children left him, and his father-in-law put a price on his head. I even had to smuggle him to another country for a short time to protect him from assassination by a fatwa of his father-in-law.

Yet none of this deterred him. He continued to be a bold witness for the Lord, and eventually God used his consistent Christian testimony to help him win back his family. Today, this man still faithfully attends the church and shares his faith unashamedly.

The courage this young man displayed was characteristic of many in the young Baghdad church. In 2008, we held a four-day revival campaign and school for pastors in Kurdistan, Northern Iraq. Just before the first service began, bombs exploded around the city killing twenty-three people. Several bombs were targeted at churches in Baghdad. To my surprise, the people of New Testament Baptist Church of Baghdad did not stay home. In spite of the threat to their safety, they made their way to church to hear the gospel. More than ten people raised their hands for salvation that day, and the next Wednesday we baptized seven new Christians—an outstanding number for Iraq.

An Extended Reach

In the beginning of 2007, I was back in the U.S., preaching for a missions conference in Powell, Tennessee, when the cell phone on my belt began vibrating repeatedly. All throughout my sermon it continued to vibrate as someone persistently tried to contact me. Afterward, I looked at the screen to discover missed calls from Baghdad. Frightened that something had happened to Pastor Maher or that insurgents had attacked the church, I rushed out of the sanctuary to return the call. Pastor Maher answered, and I felt a surge of relief that he was alive even as I asked why he was trying to reach me.

He joyfully announced that he had just received a phone call from the Minister of Communication (who happened to be a Shiite Muslim), who had told him the United Nations had asked the Iraqi government to pick eight Iraqi radio stations to represent the country in a United Nations conference held in Paris. The Minister had informed Pastor Maher that our radio station had been chosen, and the United Nations would cover travel and lodging expenses and arrange all their accommodations.

I listened in stunned amazement as Pastor Maher continued, telling me our station had been chosen because of our message to the Iraqi people, teaching the Iraqis to love one another as Jesus loves us. The Minister wanted more Iraqis to hear this positive message, and so our station represented Iraq in that international conference, and our church and radio station gained a favorable relationship with the Iraqi government. God used friendships with government officials to open new doors of opportunity to share His Word with more people of the country. It was another miracle, made possible only by our Sovereign God.

We applied to put a radio tower by the city of Basra in southern Iraq, and the government accepted. Later, we applied to widen the outreach of our station into Baghdad and its suburbs, and the government also accepted that application. We were also granted permission to establish a third tower in Mosul, the ancient city of Nineveh, enabling us to reach five million people in northern Iraq. In the midst of war, violence, car bombs, and suicide bombings, the beautiful melody of the gospel pierces through negativity and darkness through our radio programming, praising the Prince of Peace and the

Everlasting Father and preaching the message that Jesus, the Hope of nations and the Lover of mankind, still saves.

Today, wars and uprisings continue to spread throughout the Middle East. People living in the States hear of Muslims killing Muslims, rebellions everywhere, and ISIS exacting judgment on Christians with beheadings and mass murders. Terrorists and Islamic extremist organizations attack U.S. troops and their allies weekly. Yet in the midst of all this violence, many, many people are still coming to Christ. Many Muslims who are tired of the violence and bloodshed are seeking the Bible, desiring to know more about the Prince of Peace, the Lord Jesus Christ. I am so blessed to have been able to participate in this ministry and to be able to say, like the Psalmist, "As for God, his way is perfect: the word of the Lord is tried: he is a buckler to all those that trust in him" (Psalm 18:30).

FORWARD AT
THE CROSSROADS

Since my teenage years, two groups of Bible verses have always intrigued me. One group says that man has two choices: life or death. The other verses state that all things work together for good, that we are created unto good works, and God predestines His children to be conformed to His image. As a young Christian I wondered how it was possible to reconcile these two groups of verses. I concluded that God has given every human being a free will, and even though the Lord has given us through His Word many warnings and every instruction we need to make good choices, we are ultimately responsible to choose, and we alone will bear the consequences of our choices.

The way I see it, once we are born, we join the rest of the human race on the path of life, confined to the limitations of time, destined to encounter various crossroads along the way. At each crossroad, we must make a decision, whether actively or passively, and each decision affects the remainder of our path through life.

We have many examples in the Bible of those who were faced with crossroad decisions. Adam and Eve were given the responsibility to heed God's warning to never eat of the fruit of the tree of the knowledge of good and evil, but He did not stop them from making the choice to disobey. Not only did that choice affect the remaining years of their lives on earth, but it also affected the entire human race. Cain was warned about the consequences of his uncontrolled anger, but when he reached that crossroads, instead of confessing the sin of not yielding to God and offering a blood sacrifice as ordained by God, he chose to vent his anger and jealousy by killing his brother. This choice affected his relationship with God and altered the direction of his life, causing him to be an outcast from his family, destined to live with the unrelieved shame of his sin.

Jacob also faced a crucial crossroads that affected the direction of his life. Unwilling to wait for God to keep His Word and fulfill the prophecy made when Jacob was born—that Jacob would carry the patriarchal promise and the elder would serve the younger—he chose to steal the blessing and the birthright from his brother. His scheming led to divisions at home, discord between the brothers, and heartbreak for his father. Finally, he was forced to flee to the home of an uncle who proved to be just as wily as he. Jacob's choice cost him dearly and resulted in subsequent grief at the rebellion of his own children.

King David faced several crossroads in the course of his life. He knew God had anointed him to be king over Israel and unlike Jacob, he waited patiently for the Lord to fulfill His promise. In

His own time, God removed Saul and his family from the throne and exalted David to rule over His people Israel. The Scripture is careful to record the benefits reaped by David in his obedience. As long as he followed God's plan for his life, peace and success resulted. Sadly, David's next crossroads was not marked by a victory. While his army was fighting the Ammonites, David lingered behind in his palace, setting the scene for him to see the beautiful Bathsheba naked and bathing from his roof. Once again, David had a choice before him, but his wrong choice resulted in a significant scandal, the consequent murder of Bathsheba's husband, Uriah, and many heartaches. Although he later repented and asked God's forgiveness, he could never undo the decision he made.

At the age of seven, I encountered a crossroad and chose to receive Christ as my Saviour. This decision affected the entirety of my life, including my choices during other crossroads moments. My 1975 crossroad was the decision to remain in Lebanon and go through the war with my parents or leave my native country, trusting the Lord to guide me. In 1983, I encountered a crossroad decision to stay in Canada where my wife and I were comfortable or return to Lebanon with my family and follow God's call to serve as a missionary. Because of my choices at these crossroads, the Lord has blessed me with the fruit of many ministries in the Middle East and beyond.

Whenever we face a crossroad and must make a decision that will affect the direction of our lives, we should pause to consider whether our choice will please the Lord, for if we put the Lord first in our lives, we will surely experience His blessings on our lives.

Jesus said in Matthew 6:33, "But seek ye first the kingdom of God, and his righteousness; and all these things shall be added unto you." The day will come when all the money we have made, all the degrees we have earned, all the success we have achieved, and all the fame we have gained will become meaningless. All that will matter is what we have done for the Lord.

With this in mind, I look back on the story of my life and ministry with joy. From the night of my salvation until now, I can testify that God has never left me, which makes Hebrews 13:5–6 fitting life verses: "Let your conversation be without covetousness; and be content with such things as ye have: for he hath said, I will never leave thee, nor forsake thee. So that we may boldly say, The Lord is my helper, and I will not fear what man shall do unto me."

I began this story with the example of the Apostle Paul. Like Paul, I have experienced many difficulties and challenges over my decades of ministry. Looking back on my life, I find many occasions on which I could empathize with Paul when he wrote, "We are troubled on every side, yet not distressed; we are perplexed, but not in despair; Persecuted, but not forsaken; cast down, but not destroyed" (2 Corinthians 4:8–9) and "For we wrestle not against flesh and blood, but against principalities, against powers, against the rulers of the darkness of this world, against spiritual wickedness in high places" (Ephesians 6:12).

My prayer and heart's desire is to be an imitator of the Apostle Paul. Paul finished his race successfully, but mine is still in progress. There are yet more battles to fight, more souls to win, more churches to plant, and more countries to open to the gospel. I continue to run the race for God's glory. As I run, my goal is that when my life comes to an end and I stand before the judgment seat of Christ, I, like Paul, will be able to say, "I have fought a good fight, I have finished my course, I have kept the faith" (2 Timothy 4:7).

Until then, I continue to press forward.

Acknowledgements

I am eternally thankful for Mr. and Mrs. Clyde Agnes who came to Lebanon as missionaries in the mid 1950s and led my family and me to Christ and for the Christians around the world who prayed for us during the Lebanese War.

I would also like to gave a special thanks to Mr. and Mrs. Dick Knox who were missionaries to the island of Cyprus. They often hosted us in their home when we would have to flee Lebanon due to battles. In their home, we always felt welcome and found comfort.

I thank the Lord for using a pastor's wife, Mrs. Fred Daniels, who after hearing my testimony and reading my reports, suggested that I put my life story in a book. I am also grateful for many of my dear friends who graciously read the manuscript. They were not only a great help, but they were also a great encouragement. I also want to thank Lesley Gonzalez for her work in editing this manuscript and making it convey my heart.

A special thanks belongs to my wife, Rosann, who left the comfort and security of all she had known to go with me to Lebanon in the midst of a war. Through the years, she has stood by my side in prayer, encouragement, and ministry. It was her support through the writing of this book that made it a reality.

About the Author

Dr. Edgar Feghaly was saved in Beirut, Lebanon, in 1949 after hearing the gospel through the efforts of American missionaries. He immediately began serving the Lord as a young person and was called to preach as a young adult. After a brief time in the States for training, Dr. Feghaly returned to Lebanon with his wife Rosann, where they served the Lord throughout the Lebanese War and beyond. As doors opened throughout the Middle East and West Africa, the Lord has used Dr. Feghaly to plant churches in these Muslim regions. The Feghalys continue to train and labor alongside national pastors throughout the 10/40 window and are seeing the Lord work through their ministry in miraculous ways.

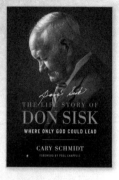
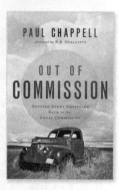

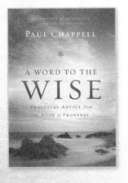

Visit us online

strivingtogether.com

wcbc.edu